The Way of Anthroposophy

Some Answers to Modern Questions

Stewart C. Easton

D1798276

Rudolf Steiner Press

LONDON

1985

ISBN 0 85440 464 3

Published by
Rudolf Steiner Press
London

Printed in Great Britain by
Whitstable Litho Ltd., Whitstable, Kent

ZMS.

Contents

Acknowledgement

THE IDEA for this book originated with Frances Woolls, a long time teacher of science at Wynstones School and devoted student of the work of Rudolf Steiner. When I started to write it I sent her each chapter as it was written, and she at once responded with criticisms and suggestions. The book as it now appears is the product of a flawless collaboration between us, aided in its last stages by valuable comments from its editor, Simon Crosby, who was also to have been its publisher, but was prevented by circumstances beyond his control from completing the work he had begun.

It is my hope that the work will serve the purpose Frances had in mind when she proposed it to me many years ago, and that it will reach the public that she and I always thought would be ready for it – an enquiring public that is asking pertinent questions, some of which we have tried to answer here.

The footnotes are mostly for the non-specialist; those initialled SC have been added by the editor, otherwise they are by the author.

STEWART C. EASTON

Chapter One

Are we only superior animals?

It is a peculiar feature of our present twentieth century that the ideas of what is today usually called, quite simply, science (in earlier centuries 'natural' science) are so much taken for granted, at least in the western world, that we do not often remember how very recent is the scientific world view. Throughout much of the second half of the nineteenth century a battle was raging between science and religion, especially over the question of the origin of man. Was the Bible correct when it pictured man as having been created by God, in God's own image (whatever that meant), or was what had come to be regarded as the scientific view, true, that men had evolved, without any guidance from God, from lower forms of animal life?

For most of the present century the battle has no longer been quite so heated. Every so often it warms up again, mainly as a result of the renewed activity of some fundamentalist religious sect. But for the most part, as far as the average man is concerned, the battle is over. The victory was to science. This was not because the religions and holders of the older traditional religious ideas ever accepted their defeat, but because the ideas put forward by science simply became a part of western man's subconscious beliefs, no longer questioned by his conscious mind.

However, the absence of overt attacks on religion did not mean that religion was flourishing and science taking a back seat. It meant only that the religious outlook on life, characteristic of much earlier centuries, had become extremely rare in our century, whereas various popular notions supposedly deriving from science have taken possession of the vast majority of men and women in the west. Irrespective of whether people go to church or not, they are unlikely to think of man as a spiritual being, a being of body, soul, *and spirit,* as was once held to be true by Christians – even if they think of him as a being of body and soul. The word soul, if used at all, is likely to be used in its Greek form as 'psyche', or, more remotely in compounds like psychology, which the average man does not connect with the word soul at all. He finds it much more comfortable to speak of body and 'mind', since the mind, as we shall see, is without religious connotations, and can be used simply as a convenient word to cover all mental activities without the necessity of having to define it.

How then does the average man regard the human being, if he does not look upon him as a being of body, soul and spirit? He is, first of all, an animal. He is descended from lower animals. Apes are his distant cousins left behind in evolution while man progressed, gradually acquiring a 'mind' when his brain had evolved so that it could engage in independent thinking. His body also evolved so that eventually he could stand upright, walk on two legs and articulate words. The average man may not even give a thought to this process of evolution in any detail, but he is likely to have heard of the Darwinian theory of the 'survival of the fittest'. He takes it for granted that man has been able to reach his present eminence by virtue of his mind, through which he has been able to outdistance the non-thinking animal world and create human civilizations totally different in kind from any of the societies created by animals, birds, or insects. Nevertheless man still retains his animal nature, and numerous characteristics that survive from earlier times before he had become *homo sapiens;* it is therefore quite unusual to hear him spoken of by the average man as if he were anything beyond the animal. He may be called

3

a social, or a political animal, and it is even thought that much can be learned about man by studying the habits of animals. It is regarded by all (except a tiny minority of scientific investigators) as entirely legitimate, as well as a scientifically impeccable procedure, to experiment on animals in order to learn about human diseases and how to treat them – and it cannot be denied that much has indeed been learned from such experiments. It is only very seldom that a scientist ever asks the question, what is the essential difference between the animal on which I am experimenting, and a human being? Or, will the medicament that I am using on the animal act in just the same way on a human being? And if not, why not?

So to the average man a human being is a superior animal – superior, as Aristotle put it, because of his *rationality*, the specific difference, as he thought, between man and animal. So for most people it is not necessary to take seriously any other possible origin, including the notion that he was 'created' by 'God' or by other divine beings. Nor is it necessary any longer to suppose that God can be interested in the behaviour of man on earth. Indeed, God has virtually disappeared as the *cause* of any earthly phenomena. Perhaps a God brought it all into being, but, as far as practical life is concerned such facts, even if true, can be disregarded. It is generally agreed that what we need now is to discover the laws of nature, how nature acts, and see how we can use our knowledge of nature to improve the quality of our lives. We cannot, of course, postpone death indefinitely, but even that may yet be achieved by men of science as they grow ever more clever, accumulate ever more facts and understand ever more of the laws of nature. Laws of nature cannot be broken, for every perceptible phenomenon on earth there must be a cause, and if we expend enough effort this cause in the end surely will be discovered. Geneticists believe themselves to be already close to discovering how to create more perfect human beings. Who knows what the next great scientific breakthrough will be, or how soon it will come?

Such ideas in the last century have become the common possession of western mankind, and they have largely pushed out all older ideas. The viewpoint known as 'materialism' has quickly and without the fuss of having openly to combat the older philosophies and religions, taken over almost all of us. Even if we verbally acknowledge the existence of God, even if we agree with our local clergyman's assertion that there is another world than ours (that he is likely to call the 'kingdom of heaven'), as a practical matter we never take it into consideration. We prefer to live as if the earthly world and the visible universe were the only worlds there are. When the same clergyman tells us that our soul (whatever that may be) survives death and betakes itself to 'heaven', that assertion may possibly interest us because most of us maintain at least some hope that death is not the end of everything for us, our family and friends.

All the same, we are not very likely to believe that what he tells us is literally true. After all, weren't such ideas handed down by tradition? Did they not originate with men who had the same kind of minds and the same kind of knowledge as we, and so did not really *know* anything about life after death or the kingdom of heaven? They speculated about them just as we do, and wrote down their speculations with more confidence than we in our own time would think of doing. Thus reason has largely triumphed over faith, though faith may persist in enough souls to keep a fair number of churches filled on Sundays; and some of the faithful may think about their faith also during the week.

So whatever the nature and depth of our beliefs, most of us are caught up by the tide of materialism and as a practical matter confine almost all our thought and our activities to the earthly material world. But *if* we do for any reason decide to think about our life on earth and whether the ideas put forward by science satisfy us, we are likely to find that they are very far from doing so. There seems to be more in us than can be truly explained by any of the sciences we know of. Even the comparatively recent and highly popular study of psychology, which does indeed purport to study the 'soul', manages to survive very well as a medical or paramedical speciality with the very minimum of actual knowledge. Some of the practitioners do not even believe in the psyche or soul that is supposed to be the object of study. Psychologists like to be considered men of science too, and its pioneers have invented new words to describe how the 'mind' functions, and how our emotions disturb our rationality below the threshold of consciousness, and the like. Other schools of psychology confine themselves to the study of the behaviour of animals, and try to fit all human behaviour into the same framework. In the process they come to regard us all as superior animals, lacking any central core capable of free and independent action.

Yet, even after reading a ponderous tome that tries to prove how we are either superior animals, or from a different point of view, imperfect machines, do we not *still* say to ourselves that we are something more than that? When we contemplate a Raphael Madonna, or hear the ninth symphony of Beethoven, or the eighth of Bruckner, something seems to stir in the depth of our being. Somehow we seem to feel better, even strengthened, by these works of art. Can it really be that it is the same process at work as when an animal salivates at the sound of a bell, indicating that one of its desires is about to be satisfied? Even if the process is recognizably similar, it is surely not *the same,* as the behaviourists would claim. What can it be that does indeed stir in the depths of our being?

It is very easy in our affluent societies of the west to allow ourselves to accept what appears to be the normal and usual values of these societies. To enjoy all the fruits of our science and technology, to content ourselves with possessing ever more and more objects, of which we may or may not have any real need, to turn on the radio or television to entertain us when we come home after a day's work, or when we have safely packed the children off to school. It is easy to avoid doing any thinking of our own when there are professionals paid to think for us, who will tell us what to think, and at the same time provide us with a carefully selected group of facts to support their viewpoint. What does it *matter* if we are manipulated by the thoughts and ideas of others? Would our own true opinion, if we had one, be any more convincing, more, as we say, objective, than what we hear on the radio, see on the television? If we were in charge of public affairs do we suppose we would do any better than the politicians we elect, whom we pay to 'represent' us – act, that is, instead of us? Of course we pay too much in taxes for the services provided us, but after all, in spite of taxes, inflation and other supposed ills, we find (if we are employed) that our purchasing power continues to increase. More goods (goodies) can be bought this year than last even if we may be a little more heavily indebted. We can even buy a foreign car if we want, possibly contributing to the unemployment of some people we know, or know of. It is easy to dismiss alarmist reports about the state of our country and the world – we know, don't we, that newspapers have to be sold, audiences have to be entertained, or at least diverted. As far as our own lives are concerned, don't we find that society is tolerably stable and the boat moves smoothly along – why should we rock it?

If we were merely a superior kind of animal, attached to nothing but our own comfort, with our life centred on ourselves and our immediate family and friends, and having a definite life-span, why ever should we want to rock the boat? Why does it sometimes occur to us that we are leading a useless life, centred only on our own self, that a self-ish way of living is not quite worthy of our selves, as at bottom we know ourselves to be? When we are depressed or ill or both we may very well put such questions to ourselves. At the first onset of physical discomfort or pain did we not rush, like everyone else, to a professional paid to look after our health, and did he not give us a medicament created for the express purpose of alleviating our symptoms? If it was successful and the symptom disappeared (or was suppressed) we thought no more about it. But sometimes it does not work, our temperature begins to rise, and we have a fever. The doctor appears again, prescribes an antibiotic, pills or injections. Slowly we begin to recover, perhaps cured by the antibiotic, perhaps not. But we have had a few days in bed, looked after by others, and we have suffered (heaven help us!) discomfort, and it has made us think – not only about our own suffering but about the suffering that is endemic throughout the world. We have *sympathized* with others who suffer, who were not able to be cured by antibiotics because there weren't any there, or they were too expensive for the sufferer to buy. Could a superior animal have experienced such sympathy? Or are we superior to the animals just because we could have a thought like that, a surge of sympathy for someone we have never seen?

When we hear the news and see what is happening to other men and women in other parts of the world, some of us may feel badly about it and wish it were otherwise. We may even wish we could help in some way. Some of us even *do* decide to help, even to the extent that we agree actually to become uncomfortable. Why? What is it in at least some of us that makes us a little ashamed of the life we lead, so free from any kind of danger or serious pain? If we were only superior animals we should no more care about other people, at least people beyond our immediate family, than animals do. But not only do we think sometimes about people less fortunate than ourselves, we also sometimes feel *with* them. We grow angry at injustice, even if it is not directed against us, we suffer when we hear of children dying of malnutrition, we are unhappy when we read of wars and massacres and tortures, even though we are not personally affected by them. Perhaps we may ask ourselves why we should be so privileged as to have been born in the prosperous west. Can we honestly say we have *deserved* to be born here? And if so, what did we do to deserve it, and when?

Before we think about such questions and try to offer some answers to them, let us first make some enquiries about ourselves, we who are asking the questions? Could a superior ape, or an intricate and complicated machine put questions like these? The machine might answer if it were 'programmed' to do so. But then some human being first would have thought up the question and built the answer into his machine – an answer that would have taken into account numerous variables, all supplied by the programmer. Our answer to the first question must therefore be no. Neither the ape, nor the machine, could have said to itself, or even thought on its own, that it was privileged beyond its merits; nor would it have cried out against an injustice inflicted on others. There must be some entity to pose these questions – we call it 'I' or give it the Greco-Latin name of *ego*. What is this 'I' of which we are intuitively aware? How is it related to our physical body?

Our physical body is made up of many physical and chemical constituents. We also say that it is alive. When some mysterious process occurs which we call death – and it is very mysterious because we all know *when* it happens (to someone else), but we do not know exactly *what* happens – this physical body at first becomes rigid, then relaxes. After a while it begins to decay, and is in no way distinguishable from its constituent elements drawn from the earth. If we could see the body as it decayed, would we still say that it was 'I', that we *were* that body? Would it not be better to regard it as a kind of house in which *we* had once lived, a house that was now disintegrating? Indeed, in our dreams we often picture our body in the form of a house, or sometimes a vehicle, which in our dreams we can enter or leave at will. So what was the mysterious entity that we call life that once animated that body of ours? And if life has left it, where has it gone? If it were still filling and animating that body, would *we* be still present in it? And we, whom we imagine now to be thinking about that house, that dead body that once we inhabited, how are we able to think about it at all? While we are, as we say, alive, inhabiting that body, we can think. Whether we shall still be able to think afterwards we do not know. We can see that the brain, with its convolutions, is decaying like the rest of the body; so obviously if one thinks with the brain one would no longer be able to think. No, we don't think with the brain, we may be told – we think with our *mind*. But what is that mind? Has anyone ever seen it, heard it, touched it? Haven't we *invented* the mind as an entity that must exist because it is needed in order to explain how we think? If so, then its existence is for ever unprovable. We think, we feel, we even will, and all these are perhaps functions of our mind – if only we knew what a mind is. But for some reason the word mind, even though we know it is only a convenient term to cover our various 'mental' activities, is more acceptable than the word invented by the Greeks: *psyche* or soul. This has ceased to be scientifically respectable. Does the soul really exist, and if so does it, as certain religions suggest, survive death, thereby even making it possible for the decaying body to be surveyed from outside by some entity with which we can identify ourselves – our 'I'?

This is a suitable point to discuss the ideas of Rudolf Steiner, ideas to which this little book is devoted. I do not wish to put him forward as an omniscient teacher with the answers to all the questions we might want to ask. But there would be no point in quoting his ideas at all – or in writing this book – if I did not think not only that they are good ideas, but that they derive from a kind of perception that in our age has become very rare; though Steiner assures us that in an earlier, pre-scientific age it was widespread. More will be said about this in a later chapter. Here all that needs to be said is that, according to Steiner, there is a world of spirit that interpenetrates our physical world, and that it can be known through the exercise of faculties that in our time are not usually active. In our age these faculties have to be developed, and there are definite stages in this 'higher' development.

I do not propose here to try to prove the existence of this world of spirit; that has been done elsewhere. The 'anthroposophy' that appears in the title of this book claims to be a *science* of the spirit, and obviously, if there is no spirit, there can be no science of it. It is here assumed that the world of spirit does exist, and was open to the developed faculties of Rudolf Steiner. His teachings derived from this knowledge should, in my view, be taken seriously. All that is asked of the reader at this stage is that he should regard this assumption as a possibility and refrain from premature scepticism. Let him then see if what Steiner says throws any light upon the questions we are studying. I am not going to offer my own answers – which would rest upon no authority but my own – but I shall constantly be trying to interpret Steiner's teachings.

This book is not intended to be an introduction to anthroposophy, nor will it make an attempt to consider all its aspects. My purpose in writing is, as its title suggests, to say something about the relevance of anthroposophical ideas to the realities of today, and how it answers questions that are constantly being asked by serious minded persons. Other books exist that set out to be more comprehensive, including my own *Man and World in the Light of Anthroposophy*★. However, in that book no attempt is made to answer the kind of questions we shall be dealing with now. Here, we are trying to speak to people who are looking for something that goes

★That book contains a reading list at the end of each chapter together with the author's comments on each book recommended. This information will not be repeated here.

beyond the traditional religious teachings, and who do not think that modern science has all the answers – and especially not those scientists who cannot bring themselves to believe that anything exists beyond the material world they study.

This book, therefore, is written for those who are willing to consider that spirit exists, and that spiritual, non-visible worlds can be known. The writer is convinced that in these difficult times this knowledge is vital for mankind. But also he believes that it needs to be interpreted in such a way that its relevance can be seen by men and women who had previously been unaware of the very existence of anthroposophy, who may never have heard of Rudolf Steiner.

Such an interpretation, therefore, will form the content of this little book, and the first questions we shall attempt to answer is who are we? Who is it who has been asking the questions with which this chapter has been filled? What is the human I, and can it exist apart from the physical body or is it to be identified wholly with that body?

Chapter Two

Who is this being who calls himself 'I'?

The human being – threefold and fourfold

THERE IS nothing nebulous about Rudolf Steiner's concept of the human being. As perceived through supra-sensible perception we are much more complicated entities than materialists suppose us to be. From one point of view we are threefold beings. We possess a 'soul' and something that is essentially 'higher' than the soul: this Steiner calls the 'spirit'. This means that we have a threefold nature, body, soul and spirit. But also we are fourfold beings, possessing a physical body, a 'life-body', or etheric body, an astral body★, and an I or ego. The life-body leaves us at death after having animated our physical body all through our life; the astral body and ego leave us at night when we go to sleep

---

★The use of the word 'body' here is particular. Beginners are generally warned that not only is it a poor analogue but it is also misleading. In this subject almost all the terms are mere pointers, the map is not the territory. Terms like 'etheric' and 'astral' have been overworked and at times have been sensationalised through spiritualism. In anthroposophy they are used in a more sedate and precise way. For those unfamiliar with the anthroposophic use the following (very basic) explanation is offered. The etheric is the basis of forces which interpenetrate us – by which we grew, and are maintained. They act so as to preserve the physical body from dissolution. Plants also have an etheric conformation. The astral is an organism which penetrates the etheric and the physical, and by which we have consciousness. It is the bearer of our impulses, fears, attractions, repulsions and so forth. Plants do not have such an organism, but animals have a rudimentary one. Man alone has an ego. It is the individual spirit entity, the higher immortal self. Just as the etheric is closely associated with the physical so the ego relates to the astral organism by giving it permanence, through memory without which its activities would fade away. For those who wish to be thoroughly conversant with all this, the second chapter in Steiner's *Occult Science* is a good source. PE.

(as well as at death). The soul acts as a kind of mediator between the 'I', whose nature is spiritual, and the body. The astral and etheric bodies together constitute the soul. Thus we can speak of the human being as made up of body (physical), soul (etheric and astral bodies), and spirit (the ego or 'I'). After death the etheric body dissolves while the astral body remains with the ego for a period equal to about the time spent in sleeping during the life just finished. Thereafter the 'I', enriched by a kind of extract from this life, lives on in the spiritual worlds until the time comes for it to clothe itself once again in an astral, etheric, and ultimately a physical body for another life on earth.

The 'mind', as an entity, does not exist. But we do indeed think, feel and with the aid not only of our physical body but of our other three 'bodies'. During our lifetime we obviously have need of our physical body (which we shall hereafter simply call our body) in order to think, feel and act with will. But this does not mean that these capacities are dependent on our body, still less that they are functions of it. After death they are necessarily changed because of the absence of a body. Indeed, Rudolf Steiner explained in his fundamental book *Theosophy* how that part of our life of feeling that was dependent on the body feels a sense of deprivation after death because the earthly desires still persist for a time, yet no longer can be satisfied through the body. Earthly thinking, feeling and willing are all dependent on the brain. But thinking as an activity merely *makes use* of the brain; when the brain is no longer able to function after death thinking itself continues.

Man and animal – the specific difference

When we asked ourselves in the last chapter if we were merely superior animals we spoke of some of the things that human beings can do and animals cannot. But to explain the actual difference between man and animal it is necessary to make use of the terms we have just used, and see how the various 'bodies' of man function.

We share the etheric body with the entire plant world, which is as alive as we are; we share the astral body with the animals, but plants, being without feeling or desire, do not possess an astral body. The animals, however, are the very embodiment of desire. Observe a pig with his feet in the trough, and imagine his relish, a huge magnification of our own pleasure when we sit before an excellent meal. Or observe a wolf falling upon his prey, a bull charging, or a cow placidly chewing. It takes no great imagination to see the powerful feeling life which lies behind outward manifestations of the life of animals. Eventually desire ceases; it has been satisfied, and very often the animal at once goes to sleep.

When an animal feels no hunger he refrains from eating. But we human beings can eat even when we have no appetite. We can stop, look and listen when instructed to do so, we can act or refrain from acting even in conditions when all our emotions urge us to act, and act immediately. These things are possible for us as human beings because we not only have an astral body (or body of desire) like the animal, but because we have an I which has always in the course of our life to some extent *transformed* our astral body, so that it is no longer exactly the same as the astral body of an animal. And in so far as we allow our I to rule and not be pushed hither and yon by the untransformed desires in our astral body, then we can act *unselfishly*. We can do things that seem to be contrary to our material interest, we can sympathize with the sorrows of people who are in no way related to us, except in so far as they are fellow human beings. We can say to ourselves 'that is just', or 'that is unjust'. We can abhor injustice wherever we may see it, and we may love justice and admire a man who acts in accordance with our own ideas of justice.

So there is no difficulty in recognizing the kind of thing we human beings can do that animals cannot. And we can say categorically that it is my own I, the inner core of my being, that is affected by the news of horrors committed in this world of ours. The compassion and sadness that we feel is rooted in that part of our astral body that has been transformed by our I. An animal cannot transform his astral body because he has no individual I capable of transforming it, and he has therefore no possibility of experiencing compassion, even though he may have a highly developed protective instinct that is not individual to him but comes from his species and is common to all members of it.

What then is this human I, and where does it come from? What is its nature? We have mentioned briefly that it does not perish at death, and that after a longer or shorter time in the spiritual worlds it is again embodied, and passes through another life on earth. But if it did not begin its existence the first time it was born from the womb of its first mother, where did it originate in the first place? Being of a spiritual nature it could have come only from the world of spirit. Its origin must therefore – as we should have supposed even if Steiner did not confirm it – be divine; and not only does it still always bear traces of its origin, but it remains linked with the divine. To use a common metaphor the I has a spark of divinity in it; and however evil we may have become during our earthly lives, as long as we are human beings at all we have not severed this link. We always remain capable of acting in accordance with the dictates of this higher being that is our I. When Sydney Carton at the end of Dickens' *Tale of Two Cities* says that it is a "far, far better thing that I do than I have ever done before", it was when he was on the point of sacrificing his life for someone else. That was his veritable I speaking; and he knew he was atoning for all the evil he had done and the wasted life he had lived until then.

It is, indeed, beyond our power to cut ourselves off altogether from this higher I of which we possess a spark in our own personal ego. But it is entirely within our power to choose not to listen to this higher I, and to refuse to do what we know the higher I would dictate if we were but to listen.

We know it is possible for us to behave in a more 'bestial' manner than any animal. And, knowing this, we often ask why does God, if he is good, why do good divine beings if there are such, permit men to behave as they do?

Man – born to be free

The answer to such questions is so far reaching as to be beyond our ability entirely to encompass, and yet at the same time is so simple that it could be understood by everyone. First of all I prefer not to speak of God because in a sense all beings above man in the hierarchies of spiritual beings are 'gods', and the very highest conceivable spiritual being is so remote from man as to be necessarily an abstraction; whereas it is possible for us to think of spiritual beings such as angels who are really quite close to man and take a lively interest in him. The being who has been called the Christ is the highest divine being who takes part in earthly evolution, but he is not the same as the being most Christians, Jews and Muslims regard as 'God'.

As has always been known, and was only very recently forgotten, divine beings do exist, ranked in nine great hierarchies above man. But none of them is free, as man was permitted to be free, so that he might become the tenth hierarchy – the hierarchy of freedom – able out of his freedom to express love. But to endow man with freedom was not so simple. It must be possible for him to make choices, to choose between good and evil. It is impossible to suppose that divine beings (or God) should be interested in most things men do from morning to night, that they should be interested in his ingenuity, his patterns of consumption, his labour-saving devices, his gadgets, still less by his armaments – though they might be deeply concerned by the uses to which any of these things might be put. We cannot suppose that divine beings would think it so very remarkable, or praiseworthy, that men should have been able to walk on the moon, or can flash a news item around the world aided by an artificial satellite far above the earth within the space of a second or two. But that divine beings should be interested in how men use their freedom, how they treat each other with hatred or with love, even in how men feel gratitude to the divine beings who created them – these things we can indeed believe of them. And we can also, if we pursue our thought along these lines, see that it was necessary for evil to exist in the world, so that men could choose not to follow it, not to succumb to but resist it, turning purposefully toward the good.

In short, it is man's *morality,* and nothing else that is of interest to divine beings. But this morality must necessarily be grounded in human freedom. If man had been created in such a way that he was compelled to obey, that he had no choice but to be moral, he might have served a useful purpose in the universe as a *servant* of the divine beings, but as *human* beings men could never have realized their full potential. It was nevertheless a grave danger for the divine world to permit men to choose between good and evil. They might come to prefer evil to good, they might indulge their own desires at the expense of their fellow human beings, they might hate rather than love. And they might destroy the world they had been given instead of preserving it for all generations to come, perhaps improving it through the use of the talents with which they had been endowed. It was indeed a grave risk, but it was a risk the divine world chose to take so that human beings might be created with all the potentialities for good and for evil of which we have spoken. Steiner tells us that not *all* the divine beings believed it was a risk worth taking. The odds were great against man's being able to handle all he was to be given. From the beginning men were tempted by spiritual beings whose task temptation is. But in recent centuries, as ever more power and responsibility were being bestowed on man, some other divine beings began to despair of men, and doubt whether it was still possible for them to achieve their goal.

And when I come to think of it, as I sometimes do, it is difficult for me not to agree with them.

In his essence man is, as we have said, a spiritual being. But it is only on earth, on the planet provided for him by divine beings, that he can learn. He has been entrusted with the earth, which he did not and could not have created himself, and he bears the responsibility for it, so that later generations of men can use it, including himself in later incarnations. The infinite wisdom built into the world by higher beings could never be acquired by man; but he could be allowed to undertake ever more responsibilities in his own life. Higher beings who at one time guided his every action relinquished their task to him by slow degrees, as man himself, from being scarcely physical at all, became more embedded, so to speak, in his physical body and gradually took on the appearance he has today. In the process he gradually lost the clairvoyance* that had always been part of man's endowment in earlier ages. He could no longer see spiritual beings, but at the same time he began to see the earth and the kingdoms of nature very clearly. So in our time it became possible for him to deny the very existence of spiritual beings and the spiritual worlds, and to deny the spiritual part of his own nature. As early as AD 869 a Church Council defined man as a twofold being, consisting of body and soul only, the soul possessing some spiritual qualities. Thereafter in Christendom it was forbidden to speak of man as a threefold being, possessing body, soul, and spirit. The spirit was thus sent back to heaven, so to speak, where indeed it belonged.

But it had not been a part of the intention of divine beings that man should totally lose his knowledge of the spiritual and become so satisfied with the earth and all that it could

*In current use clairvoyance suggests spiritualism, mediums, prediction, and so forth. In this book, and in anthroposophy, it is used in its original sense, namely the ability to perceive the non-material realities which lie beyond our physical existence. Atavistic clairvoyance still may be found but it is not to be welcomed since it is now our task *to work* to develop higher consciousness. SC.

give him that he would deny not only his divine origin but even the divine part of his own nature. The essential thing was that he should be given his freedom, because if divine beings were to *show* their approval or disapproval directly, or if they prevented man from doing anything, then he would cease to be free. They had no wish to create automata, who could do nothing but obey, do as they were told. Yet man could not be granted an unlimited freedom at too early a stage. Preparations had to be made long in advance, and a kind of guidance in moral behaviour given to him. So Jehovah, a high ranking spiritual being was given the task of instructing one chosen people in what the gods regarded as moral behaviour for man at that stage of his development – a knowledge that as yet man did not possess within himself. The result was the Ten Commandments that were binding on all men as individual human beings, together with a series of other instructions for the behaviour of the people as a whole. This was to set them apart from other peoples, and eventually make possible the incarnation of the highest being who takes part in earthly evolution, him whom we call the Christ.

Until the incarnation, death and resurrection of the Christ there was no possibility for men to fulfil the second part of their mission, namely, to express the specifically human quality of love. Man had already been granted his freedom by Lucifer, as Steiner calls him (called in the Bible the Serpent); but Lucifer could not grant him love because it is not in Lucifer's nature to love. The gift of loving came from the Christ who sacrificed himself in a deed of divine love; and it was only from the time of what Steiner calls the 'Mystery of Golgotha' (comprising the incarnation, death and resurrection of Christ Jesus) that love was implanted in mankind as a potentiality, and it is to be brought to realization by individual man through his own freedom.

Was the 'temptation' by Lucifer to which Adam and Eve succumbed, an evil act, and if so why was it permitted? We are now back again with our key question, which will be dealt with in the next chapter. What is the role of evil in the world?

Chapter Three
The role of evil

What is evil?

WE HAVE SEEN in the last chapter why evil should exist in the world, and the purpose served by it. But we have not yet considered what it actually is, nor why what some people think of as good may be considered by others as evil. Is there any objective criterion for evil?

The oldest known mention of evil is in the first book of the Bible, in which we are given the story of the garden of Eden, and are told how the Serpent tempted Eve by promising her knowledge that would make human beings "like gods, knowing good and evil". The specific sin for which Eve and Adam were driven out of paradise was disobedience. Both had been told by God not to touch the fruit of the Tree of Knowledge, but both, under the urging of the Serpent, succumbed to the temptation.

But in an age when man is free and must create his own morality, disobedience to God's commands can no longer be the definition of sin. God no longer tells man what to do and what not to do, nor does he define evil for man. If man is to be coerced his coercion must come from within. Nor did the Christ add more commandments to the predominantly negative commandments that had come from Jehovah, given to the people of Israel by Moses. What Christ did was to give two positive commandments: to love God, and to love one's neighbour as oneself. And these commandments can be interpreted only by man himself. How ought the love of God to be expressed? In a house of worship erected for the purpose or in the silence of one's own room? And must this love be expressed aloud, or simply within one's heart? When Christ Jesus was asked (as was natural after his enunciation of the two commandments) who is my neighbour? – he answered by telling the parable of the Good Samaritan, which in effect meant: everyman is my neighbour, if he behaves like one. The Samaritan, the Gentile, was the best possible neighbour to the Jew who had 'fallen among thieves'.

Could it be therefore that evil might be the *absence of love?* This would be understandable if the reason for man's creation and freedom is so that he may express love. To hate is then an evil because it goes expressly against our nature, against the purpose for which we were created. Very few of us would condone torture, or robbery with violence. But though countless millions in the west disapprove of the murder of individuals, others make exceptions for killing in wartime. This raises at once the question of whether wars, any wars, are justified, and if so in what circumstances. More millions disapprove of slavery, which has been forbidden by all Christian nations. But is forced inequality, even forced labour, an evil? We may disapprove of greed in some circumstances, while in others it is exalted as a useful virtue helpful to the societies whose members practise it and are duly rewarded when they are successful. Perhaps all these 'evils', if such they are, could be subsumed under the general category of lovelessness, failure to care about our fellow-men, and so could be regarded as offending against the 'new commandment' of Christ Jesus. But there does not seem to be any consensus of mankind as to whether one practice or another is evil. Does this mean that we are condemned to be 'subjective' in this matter? Is it possible to find any more objective criteria? Let us see if Steiner has anything pertinent to say on the matter. He has, but it requires a good deal of thought and imagination to perceive just what he means, and how it can be applied in our lives.

He tells us that there are two kinds of evil, in most respects polar opposites, and he personifies them by giving them two traditional names – Lucifer of the Christian and Jewish tradition, and Ahriman of the Persian and Zoroastrian. It will take several pages to describe even a few of the subtleties of Steiner's understanding of evil. But in the process a number of frequently posed questions on other subjects will have been given answers, thus justifying a rather lengthy discussion.

Lucifer and Christ

Let us return to the garden of Eden. The story tells us that when God created man 'in his own image', he specifically did not grant him the permission to touch the Tree of Knowledge of good and evil. It was Lucifer who persuaded Adam and Eve to eat from this tree, thereby giving them indeed that knowledge they lacked – Lucifer's promise to Eve had been that she and Adam would be 'as gods, knowing good and evil'.

The story, of course, is true at many levels, like so many. Lucifer's success was the beginning of man's separation from the gods, and his dependence on Lucifer for his enlightenment. He endowed man with all the gifts at his disposal, which included all kinds of earthly knowledge, a limited ability to think, an appreciation of beauty – in short all those gifts that make men specifically human and distinguish them from animals. But his gifts were all directed towards helping the self to develop, and with the gifts went all the desires appropriate to them. However, Lucifer could not endow men with love because he himself did not possess it; nor could he give any of those qualities that grow out of love and are akin to it.

For this period before the Mystery of Golgotha it is not quite right to think of Lucifer as an evil being. He had a task to perform for mankind, and he performed it. But without exception his gifts could always be developed to excess,

leading one to pride and arrogance, selfishness, self centred-
ness and concentration on oneself without regard for others.
This is true even of the kind of love that alone comes from
Lucifer, 'love' founded on the senses and rooted in the astral
body rather than the love that is truly rooted in the 'I', the
selfless sacrificial love that stems from the Christ. Luciferic
love is always seen in the end to be selfish and acquisitive.

It might be helpful, and I have always found it instruc-
tive, to give some thought to the Greek civilization as it was
developed before the Mystery of Golgotha, a civilization
that we in the west have never ceased to admire. All the
achievements of this civilization spring from the influence
of Lucifer in it: the Greek sense for freedom (in the sense of
detestation of tyranny), the Greek participatory democracy
in which every free man was allowed his say as an individual, the Greek love for beauty and every form of art, the
Greek capacity for thinking in a certain kind of way which
resulted in the creation of western philosophy. Yet side by
side with the development of these gifts can be seen the
corrosive egoism of the Greeks in their public life, their
excessive emotionalism that led them to constant quarrel-
ling and warfare. It is impossible to find the least trace of
altruism in Greek life. Only in a few outstanding individuals, not typical of the people as a whole, can there be
discerned any evidence of self restraint, much less any true
ethical sense.

This was, of course, the last and greatest of the civilizations in the west prior to the Mystery of Golgotha. Almost
contemporary with the beginning of classical Greek civilization occurred the life and work in the east of Siddartha
Gautama, the Buddha. The Buddha had taught the significance of suffering and the way out of suffering together
with the virtue of compassion. But even he did not provide
a sufficient impulse to the Hindu races amongst which he
worked, through which they might have tried to alleviate
the condition of the poor and their suffering. It was different

with the coming of Christ who through his life, death, and resurrection built a truly new impulse into the world.

This was possible because Christ, unlike the Buddha, was a divine being who incarnated into the body of a human being. Because of this his deed was of a totally different dimension. Through the Mystery of Golgotha he linked the I of man with the divine I, making it possible for man to allow the Christ impulse to work within him. More will be said on this later. At this point we wish to emphasize only that this deed constituted a turning point in time (which by a wonderful intuition we commemorate in our way of dating, BC and AD). After the Mystery of Golgotha it became *possible* (as it had never been before) for men to love their fellow men as Christ had loved them. From that moment also altruism, disinterested love of and concern for our fellow-men (even those we do not know and who are not part of our family, or even of our nation) has likewise become possible. The future of the world, even its continued existence, is now dependent on the development of this virtue.

After Christ, the Luciferic impulse on earth ceased to play the part it had hitherto played in preparing man for the freedom that was to come to him through the Christ. Lucifer thus became, as he had never fully been before, a being who tempted man to evil. The freedom he had bestowed, the sense of selfhood that stemmed from him, were *necessary* preparations for the coming of Christ. But after the Mystery of Golgotha, Lucifer had lost his reason for being, and from this time onward he became one pole of the evil to which man may be tempted. Excessive concentration on the self was certainly an evil before the Mystery of Golgotha. But at that time, when the self needed to be strengthened, such a concentration was surely necessary. Lucifer retains all his power to seduce, but there is now *no need* to allow ourselves to be seduced, and no good purpose is now served by succumbing. We are able to resist because, through Christ, we can attain our freedom – while the freedom still offered by Lucifer is a delusion and leads us away from our path.

According to Steiner, since the Mystery of Golgotha, Lucifer has changed his objective. He remains the opponent of Christ, just as he once opposed the Lord God in the garden of Eden. He does not want man to be free in the sense in which Christ wills man to be free, to love in freedom, to create an ethic for himself based on the clearest possible thinking, and on love. Lucifer wants man to be free to do exactly as he wishes. He wants to seduce men by offering them all kinds of illusions so that they will be permanently dissatisfied and fall into ever more and more traps of his setting. He would like man not to be a creature of earth at all so that eventually he would be willing to remain in a kingdom of fantasy, and never have to return to the earth, on which it is his destiny to live and work. Lucifer wishes to persuade man that the past was better than the present (as perhaps it was for him!), and that we can return to it and be happy, instead of taking up our tasks and responsibilities for the future.

Ahriman and his gifts – the modern world

When Ahriman was spoken of as the polar opposite of Lucifer this was a true statement in the most literal sense of the words. Ahriman may be regarded as the lord of the earth in so far as it is material, and it is under his inspiration that men have come to be enmeshed in materialism, and to believe that nothing exists on earth except what is directly dependent on the material. The earthly world is, of course, material, but it is not only material, as Ahriman wishes us to believe. If it is objected that the atom, once believed to be a material entity something like the tiniest conceivable billiard ball, can no longer be pictured as material in any meaningful sense, and as a consequence physicists have ceased to be materialists, one can only reply that some physicists still regard their elementary particles as the 'building blocks' of the universe, while others prefer not to describe or imagine them at all. But the latter would not accept the spiritual nature of the universe*, or the spiritual origin of man any more readily than do other scientists. And they are certainly not likely to think of the world as Steiner does: as a material–physical world interpenetrated by the spiritual and *animated* by it. Few biologists are willing to accept the notion of invisible etheric formative forces active in all living organisms, simply because these forces cannot be seen and analyzed – even though no scientist would deny the existence of electricity as an invisible force, knowable only through its effects. Etheric formative forces are also known by their effects. But electricity, magnetism, and other 'forces' can be subjected to mathematical treatment, unlike the etheric forces – and that makes all the difference.

The realm of Ahriman is above all the realm of the calculable, a domain that cannot be approached by higher divine beings. Ahriman's wish is for man to become so deeply attached to the earth that he will deny his spiritual nature, that he will look upon himself as a wholly material being. That he will see the earth as a field for his practical activity, to be used in accordance with his earthly understanding – a limited understanding bestowed on him by Ahriman – which does indeed enable him to manipulate the earth. But this does not mean that he can ever wholly understand it, through an intellect dominated by Ahriman. Before the Mystery of Golgotha Ahriman was not as active as Lucifer, in large part because men had not yet developed the intellect, nor the capacity for analytical reasoning.

*But some appear to be moving steadily towards it. The writings of a few of these have recently been published in a reader edited by Ken Wilber: *The Holographic Paradigm* (Routledge & Kegan Paul, 1983). This is largely devoted to the ideas of David Bohm (Birkbeck Professor of Theoretical Physics). Bohm's formulation of 'the implicate order' is tantalisingly close to being in accord with several anthroposophic concepts; see his *Wholeness and the Implicate Order*, (Routledge & Kegan Paul, 1981). sc.

In those earlier ages the earth was never entirely real to man, and thinking, at least until the Greeks, was qualitatively different from our own. Our intellectual type of thought was developed for the first time by Roman and Greek thinkers during the period of the Roman Empire. But it did not become a powerful instrument for the (limited) understanding of the world until men had completely lost the clairvoyance with which at one time all had been endowed. Later human beings became able not only to think abstractly, but also to create an abstract mathematics that could be used as an instrument to change the given world in accordance with their ideas.

It was, of course, entirely right for men to develop the capacity for calculation and analytical thinking, even though these were gifts of Ahriman. The divine beings responsible for human evolution yielded up these powers to men with the full knowledge that Ahriman could reap the harvest for himself – if he could persuade men to *become obsessed* with them. Ahriman wishes us to believe that the realm of knowledge that scientists can grasp is *all that there is* – that the physical-material is the only reality and all else is illusion. For Ahriman wants the earth to become a dead planet, peopled by men of the utmost cleverness, but inspired by him, chained to the earth and doing his will. Yet, within limits, Ahriman's gifts, like Lucifer's are legitimate, and *ought* to be used by men. But men must not be enslaved by them. Our willingness to be enslaved by Ahriman's gifts, in particular, and our growing dependence on them, have the effect of diverting us from our true goals. The attitude induced in us by our consistent and almost exclusive use of what comes to us from him, leads us into one of the deadliest of the deadly sins, that is too rarely recognized as such. I refer to what used to be called 'sloth' – laziness, a child of excessive comfort. A large part of the western world is surely sinking into sloth. It accepts passively everything that can be obtained with the least possible effort, scarcely even bothering to think of how nearly all Ahriman's gifts *could* be used actively and constructively for the benefit of mankind – and incidentally of ourselves. For example, when we use a labour-saving device that is perfectly justifiable to save us from the drudgery that used to be the lot of so many men and women, we should also pose the legitimate question to ourselves, and all other users – what do we do with the time we save? If by using computers we are spared the hard labour of using our brain/mind to make our calculations, again one may ask – to what end? Our ability to calculate, learned with such effort at school, is likely to atrophy. What do we gain in return? Computers and other products of the micro-chip revolution may take over operations previously performed by many individual skilled workers, who may be laid off work (and, not improbably, be unable to find any other). Now that it is possible to make flight reservations and hotel reservations within a delay of a few seconds, it is certainly more convenient and comfortable for us, and it facilitates travel, especially for numerous businessmen. But is it really true that what the businessman accomplishes on his distant travels justifies all this inventiveness and effort? Is the real function of business – manufacturing, producing and distributing – so greatly improved by it? Are our products so much better than before? Can it also be said with truth that any great world purposes are served by the meetings of politicians 'at the summit' and that their deliberations (if that is the word) have proved more helpful to the world than the rare and special meetings of the past?

These questions are not necessarily all intended to be regarded as rhetorical, with the answer always in the negative. My purpose in putting them forward is to remind us that Ahriman's gifts must always be regarded with suspicion, and used only after due consideration. If, for example, a major disaster occurs in a remote part of the world, and the rich nations of the west decide to use all their available resources to help; and if we use a computer to tell us where supplies can be located and what transport is available to take them – well and good – the computer has proved itself to be a good servant serving a good end. A more doubtful case might be the use of high fidelity electronic equipment to enable us to listen to good music whenever we feel like it. We may become addicted to it so that as soon as we return from work we must immediately listen to such music. It may be that this problem is more complex than we imagine; we may need to make a distinction between the effect on our nervous system of electronic (dead) sound, and the live sound that also might have been available the same evening – but perhaps played by an inferior orchestra and requiring us to move from our armchair. No one is authorized to decide such matters for anyone else, but we all ought to be aware of what we are doing. And it is most urgent that we indeed *think* instead of slothfully following the easiest path and allowing ourselves to be enslaved by our pleasures and our comfort.

The attitude towards the gifts of Ahriman is largely a question of becoming conscious of our dependence on him. His gifts always carry a price tag, which we should consciously decide we are willing to pay. Obviously we should be failing to make proper use of such things if, for example, we simply refused to use electricity. It is our destiny to have been born into this modern world that has been moulded so largely by Ahriman. And if we were to rebel against this whole modern world just because of Ahriman's influence in it, no doubt we should be in deep trouble at once, and might quickly enough land in Lucifer's arms instead. We should also be fully aware that Ahriman, as well as having gifts at his disposal, also has weapons. He is trying to prevent humanity from reaching its goal and to enslave men, to tie them to him and to a dead earth that he hopes mankind will destroy for him. Among other things Ahriman is also the lord of death, and he exercises his power over death in full accord with the wishes of the divine beings who preside over humanity. If we did not die but were condemned, like the Wandering Jew, to go on living on the earth, growing ever older and more decrepit but unable to die, this would be a sad fate indeed. And so we must be grateful to Ahriman for seeing to it that we die, sometimes even prematurely, in accordance with our karma. But the earth should not be made to lose all its life forces. It is not the intention of divine beings that the earth should become incapable of bearing life on it. This planet of ours is to be used by all generations to come, and when Ahriman (with our help) works at destroying the earth, he is no longer exercising a legitimate power.

Ahriman is also the lord of earthly power. Whenever and wherever earthly power and physical coercion are used, there Ahriman is at work. Even when in our private lives we force someone else to do our will, Ahriman is working through us. Every man and woman who wields earthly power has a particularly difficult task to avoid exercising it for ends willed by Ahriman, using means provided by him. Within Ahriman there is no devotion to truth. Every lie is inspired by him (or by Ahriman and Lucifer together) and it is possible to discern which men and women are under Ahriman's malign influence by whether they have or have not any devotion to the truth – above all when lies are deliberately used, as they so often are, to gain power, or money. Money and possessions are both gifts and weapons of Ahriman. Though money is of course nothing in itself, Ahriman has persuaded men that it is something worth pursuing, even to the point of obsession. Often money is pursued as a means to power, not only to enjoy the possessions that can be bought with it but also so as to dominate others and bend them to our will. Almost all wars in our present age are brought about by those who, while exercising power in the world, have themselves fallen into the power of Ahriman. Often their judgement has been clouded and they may have been deceived by the myriads of lies uttered during the preliminary maneouverings which precede the actual outbreak of war. Such men have ceased to be able to distinguish the truth from the lie. Ever more destructive and 'devilish' instruments of war are produced through the ingenuity of scientists and inventors, all with the encouragement of Ahriman. He it is who seductively influences our political masters and ensures the clouding of their judgement through smokescreens of lies and deceit.

Without labouring such points any further it should be obvious that the present influence of Ahriman is greater now than it has ever been. There is a spiritual reason for this, revealed by Steiner, and this reason we shall be discussing from several points of view in the next chapters. Not until long after the Mystery of Golgotha could men think their own *original* thoughts. Their thinking consisted of receiving thoughts revealed to them by higher beings. These thoughts of higher beings constitute what Steiner calls the 'cosmic intelligence'. And this intelligence was not to be entrusted to man until he had developed at least the possibility of using it wisely. If he were to become free it was of course essential for him to be able to think his own thoughts, and for this reason the cosmic intelligence had eventually to be entrusted to him. But from the moment that this intelligence became human, Ahriman also became able to influence human thinking with *his* thinking. Ahriman, the lord of death, treats everything as if it were dead; he can understand fully only the mineral world. This is also true of the scientist influenced by Ahriman. He will use exactly the same kind of analytical thinking, whether he is dealing with the organic or the inorganic world*. In other words, if he is to work with the living world he has first to 'kill' it, reduce it to ash and weigh it, or make a slide from an

---

*The great German poet Goethe, who was also a scientist, pioneered a different way of studying the world of the living. In this he was followed by Steiner who edited his scientific works in his youth, and never tired of lauding and developing Goethe's work. For more on this see the section on organic nature in Steiner's *Theory of Knowledge Implicit in Goethe's World-Conception* (page 82ff in the 1940 edition).

extract of the plant by adding some mineral substance to it, and the like.

Ahriman's intelligence is, in Steiner's words, the greatest and most all-encompassing intelligence that is imaginable – as far as earthly matters are concerned. He wishes man's intelligence to become of the same nature as his. He wishes to make men clever, *diabolically* clever, and it is possible for him to make them clever if they allow their thinking to become as cold and dead as his. The particular kind of thinking that he can influence is abstract, intellectual, calculating thinking, and this is precisely the kind of thinking that must be used in modern science as it has developed hitherto, and that lies also at the basis of modern technology and engineering. However, the Mystery of Golgotha made it possible for men to achieve a different kind of thinking, a thinking permeated by the Christ impulse. Since the Mystery of Golgotha, the Christ, who will (as he told his disciples) be with men until the end of the world ages, is nevertheless faced with the determined opposition of Ahriman. As a result, and in particular during the last centuries (when men have come to believe that there is no other kind of thinking than that of the dead intellect), Ahriman has been going from strength to strength, while very few human beings have been opening themselves to the Christ impulse and allowing it to permeate them, making possible a Christ-filled morality. Such a morality, present and active within the human I, would help men determine what to do with the inventions Ahriman has provided, and even to decide whether or not a particular invention suggested by Ahriman ought ever to be produced. For example, certain kinds of weapons (invented for use in the Vietnam war, later used by the Israelis in Lebanon, and no doubt now manufactured by all the nations with access to the technology involved) can scarcely be justified by *any* morality worthy of the name. Yet their manufacture and use is defended with the aid of arguments supplied by Ahriman, in spite of the fact that innocent men, women and children are mutilated by such weapons in horrifying ways.

It is essential now that all men of good will recognize that these modern instruments of warfare come from Ahriman, who is perhaps now being supported by beings more powerful and evil than he, and that 'God' is not going to intervene and see that he and they are defeated. Men are now bearing the consequences of the relinquishing of the cosmic intelligence to them, so that they may become free and perhaps decide, from their own volition, to follow the path of good. Ahriman has by this time obtained the firmest possible hold on man's thinking, and the consequences of this can be seen on every side. As we all know, we now have the power to destroy the entire planet with which we have been entrusted. But although divine beings are ready to help if they are given the opportunity, they must now be looking down with deep sadness on man, seeing how, like the famous Gadarene swine, he is rushing down a steep slope towards his destruction. But only man can save himself; God will not stay the hand of the powerful man with his finger poised above the button which if pressed will unleash nuclear warfare. Men and women alone can reverse the tide, assured as they are that the help of the Christ is available to them if it is sought. If enough of them are awake and also are able to understand the terrible drama that is being enacted in this century; and if they are determined to resist Ahriman's temptations (without falling into the clutches of Lucifer, thus losing themselves in unreal fantasies, including the fantasy of instantaneous destruction of Ahriman and Lucifer and all their works through a sudden intervention by the Christ), then it surely is not yet too late. We do not know the extent of the spiritual power that can be wielded by relatively few men and women – with the aid of higher beings. But we have no right nor reason to suppose that they will succeed. So all we can do is start with ourselves, open our eyes and be awake – and then act in so far as we can to allow the light to penetrate into us, and the love to flow from us.

Rudolf Steiner spoke many times of this twentieth century as being the first century of an age of light, following five thousand years of a dark age (called in the east the *Kali-yuga*). But it was also to be a century during which the forces of evil would make a determined onslaught on mankind. During the *Kali-yuga* gradually all knowledge of the spiritual worlds died out among men. But once the dark age was over it again became possible, from our century onwards, for men to win spiritual knowledge for themselves – as Steiner, a precursor of the ages to come, had himself done. As a symbol of his understanding of the drama of the centuries to come Rudolf Steiner left at his death a still unfinished carving of a being he called the Representative of Mankind, a figure clearly representing the Christ, who is striding forward, holding Lucifer in check with a gesture of the upraised hand, and with Ahriman bound beneath his feet. The power and majesty of the Christ (or the Christ-filled man of the distant future) are clearly and certainly superior to that of both the evil powers combined. But I do not think it is anywhere implied (much less stated by Steiner in the teachings of anthroposophy) that mankind as a whole will *necessarily* triumph over Lucifer and Ahriman. Mankind has the *possibility* of doing so, and with the aid of Christ the *power* to do so. But it may be that in the crucial last years of this century these hindering powers will win a great victory because too many men will have succumbed to their temptations. If, some day in the future, a disaster were to happen to men now living (and to the earth itself) such that the earth became uninhabitable, then at a later time it would presumably become habitable again. And men of that epoch would once again become able to take up the task of fulfilling the mission given to them.

Why did God not make all mankind good?

In the course of this chapter a number of answers have been incidentally given to a few somewhat naive and perhaps rather obvious questions, often posed by adherents of traditional religions. For example, why did not God make all mankind good since it was within his power to do so? Since he did not do so does not this make him an evil God, or if he is not himself evil is he not at least responsible for the evil in the world? To such questions anthroposophy must give an answer somewhat along the following lines. The divine attributes of omnipotence, omniscience and all-goodness are abstractions that are derived from mundane and limited human intellectual thinking. Knowledge, power, and goodness, as understood by human beings, are human concepts that cannot be applied to divine beings. But if for the purposes of argument, we do apply human concepts and try to understand divine motivations through them, why should not God permit the existence of evil in order to enable men to develop moral strength through resisting it and choosing to pursue the good? Furthermore, if God were to load the dice, so to speak, by not making evil attractive enough, then men would not have a real choice. The deed of Christ *made it possible* for men to choose the good while at the same time leaving powerful attractions at the disposal of the tempters, and thereby a reasonable balance was established. It is possible for man to follow a middle path, a golden mean between Lucifer and Ahriman, and in so doing open himself to the light and love of Christ. By this means he can learn to love, and in loving begin to assume his responsibility for the fulfilment of the goal of mankind as envisaged by the divine world. Surely this is a nobler task than simply being good because there is no other choice – which would indeed have been the case if evil had not been permitted to exist.

Chapter Four

The evolution of consciousness

SEVERAL questions touched upon incidentally in the last chapter obviously need some clarification, and I propose now to take up some of the more important and far-reaching of them.

I said that the twentieth century is a crucial century, and referred to it as the first century of an age of light, to be distinguished from the long five thousand years of darkness, *Kali-yuga,* that preceded it. The discussion of the question of how and why an age of light has now dawned will necessarily lead us into various subjects that cannot be elucidated without the aid of the science of spirit. So I think that a notion should now be introduced that is essential for the understanding of history and of our historical past – the idea that human consciousness, and with it human thinking, has *evolved* from prehistoric times to the present. Even now it continues to evolve, and will be different in the future from what it is today.

Very far back in time all human beings were what we should today call 'clairvoyant' (see earlier footnote), that is to say, it was possible for them actually to perceive spiritual beings who are invisible to most of us today. Until quite recently this faculty was common enough, and even now it has not entirely disappeared in some remote areas. It was possible, for example, to see various elemental beings which have been called gnomes, trolls, sylphs, naiads, elves, fairies, and the like. Such beings certainly exist even if the ordinary person can no longer see them. It was also possible to perceive higher spiritual beings. The Christian church and other religions have always believed in higher beings such as angels and archangels, and the Bible mentions still higher beings such as cherubim and seraphim. The Apocalypse of St. John, the last book in the Christian Bible, is only one of many apocalypses current among the Jewish people. All of them are full of imagery that was not simply invented by St. John and other seers, but became visible to them when they were 'in the spirit', as they called it – that is, in a consciousness different from their usual one.

Since human beings could in the remote past actually perceive such higher beings as angels, archangels, and cherubim, they could not be truly 'irreligious', much less atheistic. Knowing higher beings through personal experience they were very well aware that they were divine and not human. However, these clairvoyant people of earlier ages were very far from possessing the kind of earthly senses and capacities we take for granted today. Their life was passed in a kind of dream-like consciousness. They did not as yet cultivate the earth but lived from wild plants and from hunting and fishing and similar occupations consistent with their kind of consciousness, that could not yet see the world clearly. Then came the age when for the first time men settled down and began to cultivate the earth. The beginnings of agriculture may easily be understood as the result of the change in consciousness, and the development of a new intellectual faculty that enabled men to *predict* that when a seed was sown in the ground, a plant would in due course appear. When this was seen to happen it is certain that the knowledge would be quickly passed on to other peoples who were in close contact with the first agriculturists. Thus bases for new types of civilization arose. People began to live in towns and villages, and eventually in cities, whose inhabitants would live from the surplus produce of farmers and husbandmen.

As time went on the earthly senses of men became more

acute, and their consciousness ceased to be dream-like. Gradually they became wideawake, and more like us. As the old clairvoyant knowledge faded out it was not wholly forgotten, but was preserved within certain priesthoods; in all ancient civilizations these exercised great influence. At the time when the Egyptian and Mesopotamian civilizations flourished – in the Nile delta and in the valleys of the Tigris and Euphrates – civilizations that were already ancient had survived in India and China. It was the sages of India that gave the name Kali-yuga to the period of five thousand years beginning in 3101 BC*. They called it an age of darkness because they knew that the spiritual worlds were about to be veiled from the sight of man, and that the darkness would become ever more impenetrable as the years passed.

And so it turned out. The ancient knowledge inherited from the past was in large measure preserved. But it could not be added to any longer, and the living knowledge on which it had been based ceased to be accessible even to the priesthood. Thus the old religions, all of them necessarily polytheistic because of the multiplicity of the spiritual beings that could be clairvoyantly perceived, fell into decay. When in later times the Hebrews called the peoples around them 'worshippers of idols', they were speaking the truth. By contrast their own religion was given them through inspiration. First Abraham and then Moses received it from Jehovah, who instructed them that he was the only God who was to be worshipped, though it was left to the later prophets to proclaim that Jehovah was the God of the whole earth. The law given by Jehovah to his people was in the course of time to develop into an inner-directed moral behaviour, no longer an externally imposed law enforced by Jehovah himself.

*Kali-yuga comes from Hindu chronology and is one of several yugas or epochs. It is named after Kali, the goddess of death. The date of 3101 BC is the traditional date of the death of Krishna. SC.

The first historical epoch of Kali-yuga, marked by the rise and flourishing of the Egyptian and Mesopotamian civilizations, was a period during which men were not as yet capable of speculative thought, nor did the people *think* about their religion. They tried to find out through oracles, dream interpretations, or divination what their gods wanted of them. They worshipped their gods in great ceremonies and ordained numerous festivals. Thus their souls were nourished but they cannot be said to have *thought* about their gods. The long period of some two thousand years during which these civilizations flourished Steiner called the age of the feeling or *sentient* soul; the period in Hebrew civilization between Abraham and Solomon belongs to it. Solomon himself, it will be remembered, was *granted* wisdom by God as a gift, he did not have to acquire it. Thus in a very real sense this great master of wisdom did not think for himself, nor did the great prophets who followed him. All received their inspiration directly from the spiritual worlds, and some, for example, Ezekiel spoke of how the spiritual beings of the higher hierarchies inspired them.

But during the later years of the Hebrew civilization the cosmic intelligence, of which we have spoken, began to stream down to men. For the first time men now began to think for themselves. Although the Greeks were the pioneers in the new human activity, many Jews who lived after the Babylonian captivity were also receptive to the same inflow from the world of spirit. It was because of this that they were able to create some of the later wisdom literature, much of which was attributed to Solomon. The epoch during which this human thinking became possible for the first time is given various names in anthroposophy. But because its most important aspect was probably the new kind of thinking, the usual name given to it is the *intellectual soul* epoch. It began about 747 BC, and lasted until toward the end of the Middle Ages, the approximate date of its ending being AD 1413.

About a third of this epoch had passed when the Mystery of Golgotha took place. This, as has been said already, was such a crucial incision into world history that it was a perfectly correct intuition that made the fathers of the Christian church divide all time into the years before and after the birth of Jesus Christ. The Mystery of Golgotha gave men the possibility, the opportunity, to take the Christ impulse into themselves, thus enabling them in the fullness of time to become worthy of being entrusted with the stewardship of their planet. The Christ impulse has been working actively within humanity ever since; but relatively few men and women have as yet been able to take it into themselves. It is of the utmost importance that we human beings should do this if the world is to be saved from the catastrophes that threaten it.

The Greeks and Romans and their medieval successors in the west were as capable of thinking as any men of modern times. It may be argued that Plato and Aristotle, Plotinus and Thomas Aquinas have rarely, if ever, been surpassed as pure thinkers, subtle and logical, and with a marvellous ability to make refined distinctions and clear definitions. In this kind of thinking the great masters of Roman law were their equals. But these men knew relatively little about the external world beyond what could be directly observed. They were also scarcely interested at all in *manipulating* this world, or in acquiring what Francis Bacon was later to call *useful* knowledge. In the Middle Ages there was certainly a considerable increase in useful *inventions,* some of them taken from the more developed civilizations of China, India, and from the Muslim countries. But scarcely any of these owed anything at all to theory or to planned experiments set up to demonstrate or prove theories or ideas. What we are entitled to call western modern science is *all* subsequent to 1413, and belongs therefore to the age called by Steiner the age of the *consciousness soul,* which will continue until half way through the fourth millennium AD. We are now less than a third of the way through it, but its achievements in the field of science and technology are already far more than the sum total of what was achieved before the fifteenth century. How is this to be explained?

It is the result, according to Steiner, of the fact that the intelligence that in earlier ages had been entrusted only partially to man, has now been placed entirely in his hands. As a result a new kind of consciousness has become, or is in the process of becoming, the possession of all mankind. Steiner also tells us that just about the time of the beginning of the consciousness soul era an actual change was brought about in the brains of men through the action of high spiritual beings. As a direct consequence men began *for the first time* to regard themselves as *wholly separate* from the external world. They felt that their 'I's, their egos, were, so to speak, bystanders – looking on at an 'outside' world but no longer part of it. This outside world was now quite distinct from their own inner world, the world of the I. This meant that the outside world could be *used,* manipulated by men for whatever purpose they wished. For them the outer world was not permeated by the spirit, or by spiritual beings – as had not only been thought but had actually been *experienced* by their quite recent forebears. Now, no spiritual world lay behind the earthly world. It was wholly earthly; it had its own laws, laws of nature, to which even man was subject. These 'laws' were not like human laws, to be handed down to man by higher beings, and more or less 'obeyed'. They were laws of *how* nature behaved, and as long as they were true laws, they were immutable. Iron does not suddenly dash away from a magnet at top speed, stones do not jump up into the sky. If either of these events should ever be perceived, the human investigator would examine the phenomenon with great care to see if some other law were operating on this occasion, more powerful than the usual one. It became established that laws of nature exist and are invariable; in due course they were able to be expressed in mathematical form.

This is, of course, the way Ahriman looks at the world. For him it is calculable, and its laws are mechanical ones. For him it is nonsense to speak of the earth from any other point of view. If the earth is also the body of Christ (as Christians used to believe), the sense in which this is true must necessarily be a different one. The view of the earth deriving from modern science is the only one that most western men take into consideration. The recognition that the earth is truly living, and that it is the manifestation of the spiritual within the physical, is a part of the science of spirit. When this is generally believed it is certain that an entirely different ethic will come into being and man's relationship to the earth will change fundamentally. Those who now practise biodynamic farming and husbandry in accordance with indications first given by Steiner in 1924, do indeed practise what the science of spirit reveals. They have a new ethic in relation to the external world and how to use it. But they are still only a tiny handful among the world's farmers.

The separation of man from the world, characteristic of the age of the consciousness soul, had results in all realms of life, and not only in science. Philosophers began to ask such questions as how can the 'I' know anything at all of the external world, when it has only subjective sense impressions of that world. Another consequence of the coming of the consciousness soul age has been the tendency throughout recent centuries to stress the importance of the single human individuality, who is regarded as possessing certain rights – simply because he is a human being. The typical form of government for the consciousness soul age ought therefore to be a democracy, because in a democracy each individual has the right to have his voice heard through his elected representatives. Individualism is also recognized in economic life through the capitalist system, which encourages competition between individuals. It is no part of our intention to go into detail here on any of these matters. We simply wish to make it clear that the achievements of the age of the consciousness soul have by no means been only in the realm of science and technology. What should be grasped is that the very nature of the consciousness soul age leads to the development of individualism in all its aspects, at least in the early centuries of this era. The old bonds of community are dissolving, and a new and different kind of community of free beings has not yet arisen. Such a developed community belongs to a later epoch in which the Russian people, who are now undergoing such hard trials in preparation for that age, will be the leaders. Leadership will then pass from the west to them.

Unlike in earlier ages, consciousness during the present age is not evolving further of its own accord. The new faculties that have evolved in man in the last centuries have already been given to him by higher beings, but now any higher faculties which he can attain will have to be acquired through his own efforts. But as the consciousness soul becomes ever more deeply embedded in men it will have ever greater effects on human culture. Within the 2160 years of the consciousness soul era there are, and will continue to be, various shorter epochs of time to which Steiner gave considerable importance. In academic and other circles there used to be many references made to the 'spirit of the age', or, as the Germans called it, the *Zeitgeist*. Nowadays this concept is not so common as it used to be. According to Steiner, there really is a spiritual being higher than man who in every age is the guide of humanity and who makes himself responsible for human evolution during a particular epoch of time.

We have already explained how each major epoch is marked by a new soul development. Such major epochs are associated with the movement of the sun through the various constellations of the zodiac. As has been known since antiquity the sun moves very slowly, passing through the entire zodiac in the period of approximately 25,920 years, a period usually called a platonic year after the

Greek philosopher who described it. The vernal point, in accordance with what is called the precession of the equinoxes, moves through one twelfth part of the zodiac in one twelfth of 25,920 years. The spring equinox is therefore a few seconds earlier each year than it was the year before.

Now it was pointed out earlier that the age of the sentient soul lasted for 2,160 years, as did the age of the intellectual soul (747 BC to AD 1413), and the consciousness soul age will also last for this period. During this period of 2,160 years there are seven great guides of humanity of the rank of an archangel who influence mankind in succession – not necessarily for exactly the same period of time, the average being approximately 300 years. These archangels all bear names which have always been known in occult circles, though without the information provided us by Steiner we should not have known that they are also the spiritual guides of mankind, each taking over the task for a period. The archangels are also connected with the planets, including the moon. Raphael, for example, who accompanied the young Tobias in the well-known story included in the Apocrypha, is the planetary spirit of Mercury. Gabriel, who announced the birth of Jesus to Mary is the planetary spirit of the Moon, while Michael is the planetary spirit of the Sun.

An age under the jurisdiction of Gabriel, archangel of the Moon, is always followed by an age of Michael, and in many respects these ages are polar opposites. Gabriel guided humanity from AD 1510 to 1879, and it was his task to influence men deeply in the direction of materialism. He was also concerned with everything that pertains to heredity and the hereditary principle. He fostered the tendency towards nationalism, thus softening the rather excessive individualism that we have mentioned as one of the great advances of the epoch of the consciousness soul. The solitary individual in this way can identify himself with a group, the group of his own people and race. The epidemic of nation-building characteristic of the last few hundred

45

years was therefore quite natural in an age guided by Gabriel.

But when Michael took over the leadership from Gabriel in 1879 (a position he will retain for approximately another two hundred years from the present time), mankind received an entirely different impulse from him. Michael, unlike Gabriel, is a universalist spirit, and it is his wish to lead mankind to transcend all that he received from Gabriel, to go beyond the nation-state into a new universalism and cosmopolitanism. We should replace our old national feeling by a feeling for all humanity, recognizing each man to be our brother. Some aspects of this change are fairly easily visible in recent history. This cannot be truly explained without some knowledge of the spirits who in succession guide humanity; we can also see clearly enough how badly we are falling short of the goals we should pursue, especially when we put the interests of our country (as we perceive them) above the interests of humanity, and when we continue to make distinctions on the basis of race, language, religious beliefs, and the like.

Although Michael is now, for the first time since Greek antiquity, the spirit of the age, he also has another task in the universe which has always been his, and that he never abandons. He is that spiritual being who is the special helper of the Christ; and as such has a very profound interest in the mission of man. It is Michael who has always been the administrator of the cosmic intelligence of which we have spoken. It was he who, in accordance with the intentions of beings higher than he, gradually relinquished it to man. As is well known, Michael is often pictured as the vanquisher of the 'dragon', and this holding of the 'dragon' in check in the spiritual worlds is indeed one of his tasks. From the beginning he fought against Lucifer and Ahriman, always helping man and believing in him. At one time, when men were naturally clairvoyant, Michael could be seen in the spiritual world accomplishing his task. The 'dragon' today is primarily the dragon of materialism, that materialism which denies the very existence of the world of spirit. During the age of Gabriel materialism increased and flourished, but since the age of Michael began our rightful task has been to turn away from materialism and look instead to the world of spirit.

Materialism, we should remind ourselves, has an important element of truth in it. Everything on earth has a material basis, and from this basis it is entirely proper for us to study with all the means at our disposal. Just because modern science is based on an intellect which is capable of studying and understanding only the material world, it should not be blamed for doing what it is so well fitted to do. Indeed modern materialistic science is worthy of the utmost admiration for its genuine achievements. But these, admirable as they are, give the scientists no right to deny the existence of what cannot be perceived by our five senses, or by those instruments we have invented that extend the range of the senses. What is invisible to the eye is only invisible because the eye is not the human instrument that is designed for perceiving the invisible world. Perception into this world requires the development of suprasensible faculties. A blind man gifted with active suprasensible faculties would not thereby be justified in denying the possibility of also seeing through the eyes. If an eye were described to him and all the wonders that can be seen through it, surely his proper attitude should be to express his admiration for such a faculty, while regretting that the world seen through the eye was invisible to him because of his blindness. But it would be ridiculous for him to refuse to believe in the capacities ascribed to the eye or in the objects in the external world that he cannot actually see for himself.

This would be just like a materialism which denies the spiritual; that is in our present world an evil because it ties man too closely to the earth. By this means it promotes the purposes of Ahriman, and concentrates man's attention and interest on material things, thereby denigrating those aspects of man that alone make him human – his spiritual aspirations, his capacity for disinterested love and altruism, and similar non-material aspects of his nature. Materialism emphasizes the importance of material possessions, thus *promoting* covetousness and greed; it assigns no value to self-restraint. When men and women in a materialistic age are kind, loving and thoughtful, when they show compassion for the oppressed, when they share their possessions with those who have less than they, when they possess ideals and live up to them – then these virtues demonstrate in a very real sense that they are not materialists at heart. Yet, by contrast, it is far from impossible that a man deemed religious by his fellows (because he goes to church, believes or acknowledges his belief in God, and looks forward to a blessed afterlife in heaven) may well be a *practical* materialist, always on the watch for every possibility of material gain. And he may even have an unconscious expectation that his religious observances, his prayers and his beliefs will *earn* him a place in heaven. In our day it is our task to allow the Christ impulse to enter our inner being and to do our best to help it to work within us. It is inconceivable that the Christ would be interested in our possessions any more than he engaged in their acquisition when he was on earth. Thus the refusal to believe in anything except the material world necessarily works against the Christ impulse, and Michael, who is a faithful helper of Christ, cannot make use of materialists to further his work for humanity.

But this is not to say that we should despise the material, or refuse to soil our hands by dabbling in the earthly. Nor that we should try to follow exclusively 'spiritual' aims, as we may think them to be. This would send us straight into the waiting arms of Lucifer, who tries to catch on the rebound all those who become disgusted with the ascendancy of Ahriman in today's world. Even if our ideals are spiritual it remains necessary to keep our feet on the ground where they belong. Lucifer balances out Ahriman, both are needed. And the true Christian path is equidistant from them both, a very narrow and difficult path, but illuminated by the light of Michael and the Christ.

Whereas Gabriel fostered a certain kind of individualism and focussed man's attention on the earthly world – necessary stages in the development of human freedom – Michael has a different task. He does not work against what Gabriel did so well in his time, but he wants to lead men not only to bring about the ego-development furthered by Gabriel but, in addition, the development of love for one's fellows. Such a love springs from the developed human being, whose core and centre is his I, which, when filled with the Christ impulse can love and appreciate *all* mankind. This is something different in kind from the natural love that we feel for members of our family, for our nation, or our race, and which has in it elements of gratification.

It was under the influence of the spirit of Michael that men began first to set up institutions that transcend the individual state or nation. However imperfect the League of Nations proved to be, and the United Nations has turned out to be so far (largely because of the use made of them by powerful or self-seeking nations), the ideal behind both was inspired by Michael. He is indeed, in this century, behind all forms of initiative that tend to transcend the Gabrielic institution of the nation-state. I believe that it is of great significance that since 1879, when the guidance of Gabriel came to an end, no new nations have been built that are demonstrably true nations such as the nations of Europe that were created between the Middle Ages and the end of the Gabriel age in 1879. The relinquishing of their colonies by the western powers was followed by a powerful and prolonged effort to create new nation-states on the western model. But it must surely be admitted that there is not a single case in the world where a true nation-state has indeed been created out of a former colony. Almost all of them are clearly artificial creations, and their inhabitants do not feel themselves first and foremost to be members of the new 'nation' – as a rule they continue to feel themselves members of a particular tribe or people. From the Michaelic point of view the effort to form a new nation based on an outmoded western archetype is a self conscious piece of archaism (a Luciferic anomaly) and indeed not at all in accordance with the needs of a Michaelic age.

We are now in a position to answer the first question we set ourselves at the beginning of this chapter: what is so special about our present age, and in what respects does it differ from all previous ages of the past? First of all, we are living in the age that we called the age of the consciousness soul, the first age in which it is man's task to become fully conscious of himself as an individuality and to become aware of his separateness from the outer world. Man is now able to see the outer world very clearly as separate from himself, and for this reason he can not only observe it minutely, but he can change it, and make use of it for ends that he determines for himself.

The consciousness soul age will last, as have other ages in the past, for about 2160 years guided for a little more than the next two hundred years by the highest of the archangels, Michael, the archangel of the Sun. Such an epoch is always of very special significance. In the exceptionally important Greek Classical epoch Michael was also the spirit of the age. The time has now come when we must learn to transcend the old limitations of nation, race, people, and even family, and move forward to a more universal ideal, when every man will be regarded as our brother because he shares our common humanity. We should move towards a condition when we can no longer enjoy our own happiness, can no longer even *be* happy, while any of our brothers are oppressed. We cannot reach such a condition in a moment, but we should look upon it as an ideal, the fulfilment of which is helped by the spirit of Michael, whose task is to help us to see all men as our brothers in Christ. In the next epoch, the sixth, this ideal will come to realization, but we should be preparing it here and now.

During this present age of Michael a beginning must also be made to acquire a new conscious knowledge of the spiritual world. This has become possible now because, just twenty-one years after Michael assumed the guidance of mankind, we also left an age of darkness and entered an age of light. The Kali-yuga had lasted five thousand years before coming to an end in 1899. The age of darkness received that name because during its course the old clairvoyance had come to an end. Men ceased to be able to see into the spiritual worlds as they had done in earlier ages. The darkness came upon mankind quite gradually, for at the time of the Mystery of Golgotha it was still possible for highly developed human beings to perceive spiritual beings. We remember how St. Paul on the way to Damascus was enabled, after Christ's resurrection, to see him in the etheric world. All the apostles were to some degree clairvoyant. Later, when men began to think that the spiritual worlds were simply figments of the imagination, then the reality of much that is written in the Gospels was denied. Scholars began to interpret the Gospels from a realistic, materialistic viewpoint, which reached its climax in the nineteenth century. This was 'the darkest hour before the dawn'.

Though we have now entered an age of light, this does not mean that light will simply stream from the spiritual worlds into the souls of men because the old age has come to an end. What has happened now is that it is again possible to re-acquire direct knowledge of the spiritual worlds, and thus *know* for certain of the reality of the spirit. But for a long time to come this possibility can be realized only by human beings who make the necessary effort. Rudolf Steiner has indicated the path in several of his books, but especially in his *Knowledge of the Higher Worlds*. And I hope it will also be clear why I believe it was no accident that

Steiner grew to manhood and began the first part of his mission in 1879 when he was 18, the year that Michael became spirit of the age; and that he began to speak publicly of the worlds of spirit (of which he had been aware all his life) only in 1900, the year when the new age of light began. And just at that time there appeared audiences to whom he could speak and by whom he could be understood.

The other question of supreme importance that ought to be asked before this chapter comes to an end is why do we see in this century so little evident moral progress? If Michael is guiding mankind during this century and if he is able to vanquish the dragon, as we have said, and if this age is the beginning of an age of light, ought we not to see some external signs of all this? We have had two world wars, more destructive than any known before in history, and ever since the last war ended we have been plagued by dozens of small wars. Furthermore, there has been for several decades an imminent danger that a more destructive war than any in the past will suddenly break out in which the two most heavily armed powers may be involved, and from which it seems difficult to suppose that any civilization will survive. To a truly objective observer it is senseless that these two superpowers should fight each other and thus doom all civilization. Why should these things be in the very century when we should be learning to love or at least tolerate each other, when we ought to be overcoming our dangerously excessive individualism and egoism?

As has been indicated before, the major part of the answer must be that men are now on their own, and higher beings are not willing to save mankind from its own excesses. It is not their task to *coerce* men into doing anything, or preventing them from doing anything dictated by their unbridled will. A being like Michael stands ready to *help* men if they desire it. But first they must come to know as deeply as they can the real condition of mankind at this present time. We must recognize that it is *quite impossible* for us to return to the past, to some age when things – at least as seen from our present vantage point – were much more simple and orderly, when society apparently was not in turmoil, when people supposedly thought more about their duty than their rights. Most probably the past was never quite like this, but there is always a kind of Luciferic hankering for a wonderful past that never really was. Today it is essential that we become fully aware of our own time, its needs and possibilities. It is essential that its dangers should be understood for what they are, and faced squarely. As we said before when describing the work of Lucifer and Ahriman, we must not allow ourselves to be diverted from our path once we have seen it.

Precisely because of the scientific and technological development of this century, Ahriman has been able to seize hold of men's thinking in such a way that men and women spend almost all their time talking and thinking about his devices. They talk about money, about business, about possessions and how they can be obtained, and all the resources of publicity are used by Ahriman to keep us diverted. But if material things do not attract us because of our individual temperament or because we have become sated with them, then we become wide open to the seductions of Lucifer. He weaves fantasies for us, perhaps attracting us to new forms of religion, with the offer of new spiritual powers to be acquired with the expenditure of a little effort, by meditation about 'higher things' beyond the range of ordinary people. In this century we have become especially vulnerable because, at least in the west, we are offered so much that we can accept passively that most of us do not seem to find the time or opportunity to do any serious thinking. Our life is passed amid a host of pleasures and self-imposed tasks and duties that may not be at all necessary.

As everyone is aware, this is a century during which far more men and women dispose of more resources than was ever possible in the past. Without doubt we are a consumer society, but this is not *inherently* a bad thing. It is fundamentally a good thing that more of us have more devices to save us from the drudgery that was formerly the lot of all but a fortunate few. But this makes it all the more necessary that we should constantly put the question to ourselves: what do we do with the time we save and with our freedom from drudgery? If we fully realize how privileged we are in the west, what conclusions do we draw from the realization?

I think a case can be made out that we have allowed Lucifer and Ahriman to saturate us with all that they offer and that this has led us to neglect the real task that lies before us during the rest of the period that mankind will be guided by Michael. Instead of taking charge of our destiny we human beings have allowed ourselves to drift passively, not assuming those responsibilities placed on us by higher beings when they created man to be the tenth hierarchy. We do not think enough, we do not love enough, very few of us are at all close to being true human beings. Although in this century there may well have been more true heroism of every kind, and even now great sacrifices are made by many to bring our best human ideals to realization, such followers of Michael and Christ are still, unhappily, relatively few.

It was also in this century that Rudolf Steiner took upon himself the task of helping mankind to understand, and to choose a path that will avoid the traps, pitfalls and diversions offered by Lucifer and Ahriman, a path that will be worthy of the tasks laid upon man by his creators.

Chapter Five

Our privileges as westerners: have we deserved them?

AT THE END of the last chapter a very important question was raised. Are we always aware of our exceptionally privileged position as westerners? If we personally have evolved so far that we can think with the awareness of the consciousness soul, what are we supposed to do with this capacity? Does our exceptional privilege carry with it any corresponding responsibility, and if so what is this responsibility and how should it be exercised? Lastly, and most fundamentally, is there any reason why personally we should be so privileged? Is it simply a question of lucky chance that we happened to be born in the west and have inherited all the achievements of western civilization?

Obviously as an historian and student of the contemporary world I could write many pages on the condition of the rest of the world outside western civilization, showing with numerous examples what terrible conditions are the lot of almost all other peoples, and how apparently impossible it is for any of these peoples to 'pull themselves up by their bootstraps' and by their own hard work come to share in the prosperity we ourselves possess – even if there are some flaws in it and there is still room for much improvement. Almost all countries outside western civilization suffer under tyrannous governments, and the people have no enforceable rights against them. In almost all there is a very tiny class of privileged persons who have access to consumer goods almost on the scale to which we in the west are accustomed, while the vast majority of the people never have enough to eat, and their social and political systems are such that they are never likely to overcome their disadvantages. In a few countries conditions have been improving to such an extent that there is at least no further danger of starvation. But even these countries are likely to suffer from tyrannous and authoritarian government.

In short there are very few countries indeed where the future can be regarded with much optimism. Even in those countries where the economy is functioning fairly satisfactorily and where a privileged class is growing in numbers, it may well be that the poorer classes are finding themselves more oppressed and less able to obtain access to consumer goods than they were before their economies had begun to show apparent improvement. Even in western countries, especially when these undergo an economic depression, there is everywhere an 'underclass' which cannot regard itself as in any way privileged, though their standard of living may be immensely higher than that of a poor farm labourer in Bangladesh or Mexico. If we should, as was suggested in the last chapter, regard these impoverished and dispossessed human beings in other parts of the world as our brothers, is there anything we can do, or should do, to help them in a material way?

Let us give some thought to the consumption of meat in the western world. As prosperity in the west has been growing in the last decades, so has the consumption of meat. Yet the animals bred for meat feed on an acreage which, if planted, could sustain many times more than those who feed on the carcasses. A few centuries ago it was only the surplus and aged animals which were used for food, meat eating was infrequent and some ate no meat at all. Today it has become a sign of prosperity that we can eat meat, and animals are raised specifically for the purpose of satisfying our wishes. Starvation now claims many thousands, even millions, of lives every year – should we give up meat to feed the hungry in the rest of the world? If we gave up meat could enough grain be grown to feed them?

It is not unusual to hear westerners claiming that they have deserved to be privileged because they work harder, because almost all the inventions used to increase production are western (as are most highly efficient systems for production and distribution). The argument may then go that the Communist countries should change their system to one more like the western. It is sometimes said that if the third world would imitate western methods, then with all the resources at their disposal they could eventually equal the productivity of the west and thus solve their economic problems. A similar argument is often used within the western countries to explain differences between rich and poor, the excessive privileges of quite small minorities. It is said that the unemployed and poor are inefficient, or dislike working, while the virtuous rich (or at least some of them) have reached their present pinnacle by intelligence and hard work.

Without going into the merits or demerits of such arguments, several observations could be made on the subject from an anthroposophical viewpoint. The facts are available to all, even if I interpret them from this viewpoint. The economic and political systems of the world are clearly not designed to enable the maximum number of human beings to profit from the increase in productivity and in the availability of goods that has been made possible by advances in technology – a realm in which Ahriman is strongly active. Moreover, since money itself is looked upon as a commodity instead of being a mere medium of exchange, it is possible by using money solely for speculative purposes to become richer than by simply producing useful goods. Money has become a badge of status. We even say that man is *worth* a million dollars or the like. Such wealth is sought so as to acquire power over others, as well as granting its possessor a superior social position. Ahriman is the lord of money, it is one of his most effective creations for the enslavement of mankind.

The competitiveness of the economic system operating in the west, however much it may favour productive efficiency, and however responsible it was for the great economic advances of the nineteenth century, is very far from being what is called for in an age under the guidance of Michael. The system is such that, whatever the degree of our goodwill we cannot help impoverished countries effectively. If our governments extract money from us by taxes, or if banks and governments create new money to enable these other peoples to live better, by lending or giving it to them, or even if western style business enterprises are created in the third world, it is almost invariably the western nations and their banks and shareholders that profit from them. It is now obvious to many that the capital of almost all loans to third world countries will never be repaid, and that often the interest can only be paid through more borrowing. Whilst such means of dealing with problems of undernourishment, impoverishment, and actual starvation are impossible to defend on rational grounds, nothing better has yet been found.

In the years immediately following the first World War Rudolf Steiner set forth a number of principles and practical ideas for the improvement of world conditions of that time. But unfortunately it is certain that nothing of the kind he proposed then could today be practical on a world scale. However, it seems that the old system that grew up in the age of Gabriel cannot be shored up much longer. We must suppose that any system that will eventually replace it will have to be in accord with the new needs of an age guided by Michael – if it is to function as effectively as did the old Gabrielic system. Therefore it needs to be based on the recognition that all men are brothers; that we are responsible, individually and collectively, for the welfare of mankind. For a short time after the first World War it was thought by many idealists in the west that a new fraternal system was being installed in Russia, where brotherhood was a much more acceptable ideal than in the individualistic west. But from the beginning the Russian Revolution was taken over by a group of men whose primary motivation was a determination to grasp and keep power. And so it has remained. Their economy is scarcely any less Ahrimanic than that of the west, and the efficiency of its productive and distributive system is clearly inferior*.

The Chinese model established under Mao Tse-tung after a successful revolution was in part based on Soviet experience; but its more recent modifications do not suggest that there are any new ideas inherent in it that could serve as models for the west.

If our free gifts get diverted or otherwise fail in their purposes, and if loans impoverish the debtors and enrich the lenders, what is the answer? Is there any way out of the dilemma? Gifts which are literally free (not tax-money extracted by our governments) can be of great help to alleviate suffering, and it seems to me that those organized groups which are based on Michaelic ideals deserve our utmost support; indeed the presence or absence of such ideals might well be a suitable criterion for our support. Also it is essential that we truly perceive what is happening in the word as well as individually being ready to share our personal substance with the dispossessed. This is no more than may be expected of us as Christians. In addition there are also ways of meditating and praying that have an influence on the spiritual atmosphere around the earth. Such praying and meditating should be based on a true knowledge of the present activity of the Christ and of Michael, and how they are waiting for mankind to call upon them for aid.

*According to Steiner, who had nothing but harsh words for the Bolshevik Revolution in Russia, it will not be until the sixth age, the age of the Spirit-Self, that the Russians will come into their own. Then they will take over the leadership of the world, based on the developed spirit-self which will stress the brotherhood of mankind and will overcome the individualism of the consciousness soul. The present Russian system has little to do with the soul configuration of the Russian people but the sufferings of Russian individuals may well be preparing the new humanity that is to come in that later age.

We all need to recognize, in the deepest part of our being, that we are, as stressed earlier, greatly *privileged* by comparison with many others. We personally, may even be so privileged that we have been born into a class that lives comparatively easily – of course without any apparent merit on our part. That places a responsibility upon us which we should accept gladly as an opportunity to be used for bringing our ideals to realization, at whatever cost to our comfort. If we recognize neither this responsibility nor the opportunity presented to help in the work that Michael would have us do, then indeed we have not deserved our privileges but deserve only to lose them. It is not correct to think of privilege as something that has been *merited*. In a sense it may be due to us, but not as a reward. Rather, it arises out of what we have accomplished in former lives so that now we have been placed in a position where we can help mankind onward. We can do this first by developing all those higher qualities that are latent within us, and then by using these qualities productively for the purpose of helping mankind fulfil its mission. But our privilege does not give us the least right to rest on our oars and simply *enjoy* what we have been given.

The next chapter will be dealing with the most important question: why are we where we are, and what is it that is required of us? We shall be dealing with the question of reincarnation and, above all, karma. But before we are ready to discuss that there is one very important topic that is forcing itself upon our attention – not only in the countries of the industrialized west, but also almost everywhere in the so-called 'developing' world. We have alluded once or twice in this chapter to the unemployed. They are usually classed with the poor but the two groups obviously are very far from being identical: numerous persons would remain poor even if employed because their talents and education are neither rare nor sufficiently valued by potential employers.

In the past most unemployment has been of a temporary nature: people being unemployed *between* jobs. The so-called hard core unemployed have been relatively few in number, and most states have provided them with a minimum to enable them to live without work. However, today the position has radically changed. We now have single machines which can do the work of many people and so the need for human labour has steadily decreased. If for humanitarian reasons an employer were to decide to refrain from installing the latest technology he could be sure that some competitor would do so, and maybe put him out of business. This is an iron law of the present economic system, characteristic of the western industrial countries. Because it leads inexorably to the use of labour-saving devices wherever these reduce costs, it has become ever more difficult to absorb the labour that has thereby become 'surplus'. So-called service occupations cannot be expanded indefinitely – any industry employing an excessive number of people in service jobs is likely to become uncompetitive. White-collar jobs that used to be filled by the better educated members of society are increasingly being taken over by powerful computer-based equipment, which now does much of the work formerly done by secretaries, bookkeepers and clerks of all kinds. And higher education no longer guarantees a job. In the United States, where education has always been regarded as the passport to success, thousands of men and women with PhDs are unemployed or underemployed. Many middle-class housewives would gladly employ household help if it were not so costly and scarce. So should the cost to the housewife be lowered, for example, by reducing the contribution she has to make to the social security of her employee? Is it the right answer to such problems to force marginal workers to accept work at lower wages and perhaps without social security? Would measures of this sort really solve the problem of unemployment?

As long ago as 1919 Steiner severely criticized the almost universal tendency in the west to regard human labour as a commodity, bought and paid for in exactly the same way as actual products*. In making this observation Steiner was following in the steps of other nineteenth century social critics, but his solutions were quite different. Work, he insisted, should be performed as a service to society and mankind. Work is necessary if goods are to be produced, but it does not necessarily follow that the work and the products of work have to be linked inextricably in what used to be called a cash nexus. Money plays a necessary part in the process of production and distribution. Therefore it is not improper to place a monetary value on all *goods* produced, having taken into account the labour content. But that does not necessarily mean that the labour iself has also to be valued in monetary terms. Nor does it mean that money received by workers *has to be* included in the cost of production (on which the selling price of goods may be based).

This may seem over-theoretical, but an enormously important principle is involved. If labour is *not* a commodity, then it should not be treated as such, should not be assigned a monetary value. Rather, we should see that we work because without working we cannot fulfil our task as human beings (making maximum use of our talents and capacities). This is to move away entirely from the time-clock perspective – having our hours counted by machine, and then being paid an agreed sum of money for every hour worked. Also it is a move away from the piece-work system – pay for each article produced by our work. Whether we work by the hour or at piece-work, labour and materials are equivalent in the eyes of the costing department. Thus human labour (which includes the skill and individuality of the worker – both truly without price) is equated with

*See especially his book *Towards Social Renewal,* at the end of Chapter 1, and *passim.*

material and thus becomes, as Steiner said, a commodity. But if, by contrast, a man is paid according to his needs, if he receives in money the amount he needs to lead a decent life and support his family, then his dignity as a human being is unimpaired. His humanness has been taken into account. Then we should work not so much for our living, but rather because we recognize in our hearts and minds that we *ought* to work as a part of our duty towards the earth, and towards our fellow-men who in fact work for us as we work for them. We have become so accustomed to the notion that work is paid for and that without this incentive people would not work at all, that it is difficult for us to think about it in any other way. Society in the west provides the non-worker with at least enough to eat, but social security is regarded by most people as tolerable only if it is a temporary stop-gap until a wage is again *earned*. The notion that we should all be paid according to our needs begs the all important question of what are our needs, and are the needs of all of us the same? If not, how can one differentiate them?

Steiner, being very well informed on affairs of everyday life, was undoubtedly aware that many economic questions are unanswerable in our present-day societies, under our present-day systems. Therefore he elaborated an entirely different kind of social and economic order, but as yet this has not come into existence anywhere. In such an order labour would cease to be a commodity, and all men would be granted a fair share of the goods made available by their own work and the work of others. Theoretically abundance ought to be possible for everyone if production and distribution were arranged on a rational basis. The question of who needs what and how much would then become less pressing. But the problem would remain that some jobs are less interesting than others, some more strenuous and dirty – in a free society who will choose to do which jobs, and why?

It is impracticable to discuss at length here either an

ideal society or the kind of society envisaged by Steiner. But what we can do is think seriously about such problems. The first step is to dissociate the idea of working from the idea of being employed, either to do a specific job, or being self-employed (work from which a profit·will be earned, this profit being the equivalent of a salary). By making this distinction we can begin to see that it is not inescapable that the only work that is worth money is the work that is paid for. It is also untrue that the unpaid worker necessarily does less work than a man who works for pay. The truth is that we work best, not when we are highly paid for our work, but when we 'believe' in what we are doing and regard the work itself as valuable and worth doing. Does the President of the United States receive his salary in return for work, or does the British Prime Minister? Or the creative writer who may or may not succeed in having his books published? The majority of the members of the cabinet in the United States often give up lucrative positions when they start working for the government, and accept much lower salaries.

When Karl König founded the Camphill movement (for helping retarded children according to the principles of Rudolf Steiner) he laid it down as a principle of the homes he founded that no one should receive a salary. The helpers, who are called co-workers, all receive enough money to satisfy their needs while they work in these homes. Also in the Steiner schools for normal children it has always been found impossible to match the kind of salaries paid to state teachers. Yet the teachers in Steiner schools have more work to do than state teachers, partly because of the numerous meetings they attend. These are necessary because the schools are run without the 'aid' of paid administrators. Throughout the world farmers put in long hours of work with correspondingly less financial reward than paid employees anywhere. These cases have one thing in common. Such people 'believe' in what they are doing, and they do the work because it needs to be done. The work itself demands their dedication. Seen another way, unless we are too old, too ill, or too tired, we may all fulfil ourselves by working. The person who does not do work that is, in his own eyes, worthwhile comes to regard himself as something less than a full human being; and it is not too much to say that a man who lives from his inheritance or safely invested income and who does nothing but try to 'enjoy himself' is only too likely to deteriorate. By contrast those who inherit great wealth and try to make good use of it often work harder than most, making great efforts to discover how to employ their wealth for the benefit of mankind.

Some unpalatable truths have been pointed to which will have to be faced sooner or later. Furthermore, it is almost a certainty that no country in the west will – at all events in the absence of a major war – again find itself in a condition of full employment, such as existed for a time after the last war. Nor is there the slightest indication that a new and different system will come into being by peaceful means in the west, one that would be capable of putting all the unemployed to work at regular wages. What then ought to be done about the unemployed? Nowhere in western countries are they left simply to starve; they do receive something to enable them to live. And almost everywhere governments are expending effort and money to retrain and re-educate those among the unemployed who seem likely to profit from such training. But even after training, jobs are not necessarily available, so that often older employees are replaced by younger trainees, and there is no increase in the total number of employed. It is also supposed that work could be spread more widely if more older workers retired early. But always the same assumption is made: everyone capable of working ought to be *employed*, only persons receiving a wage have any proper call on the goods and services that enable them to live. The one exception to this rule seems to be the independently rich who live from their own savings or the savings of their ancestors. Otherwise, it is commonly thought, only the retired, the gainfully employed and their dependents are properly entitled to the products provided through the collective work of all.

When, in the west, major problems of unemployment first arose (in the period between the two great wars), strenuous efforts were made, through various expedients, to put money into the hands of the unemployed. The first two Franklin D. Roosevelt administrations in the United States looked at the problem with considerable imagination. It was recognized that various social needs of the country were not being met simply because governments had not yet undertaken to meet them. So agencies were created that occupied the unemployed with conservation, building country roads, clearing waste lands, and similar projects. These agencies were allotted tax money appropriated by Congress for the express purpose of giving the unemployed something to do so that they would not simply remain idle★. Writers and geographers were given work in preparing adequate maps of the whole country and guide books were commissioned for every state in the union. But it was always thought that unemployment was a temporary phenomenon that would disappear once the economy had begun to right itself. In fact the economies of all the western countries only really recovered when the war mopped up the unemployed through the enrolment of able young men into the army and setting others to work to provide for the needs of the armed forces. After the war there was a huge backlog of work and a long period of expansion followed, which has only very recently ground to a halt – so recently that there are still optimists who continue to believe that, with the aid of public expenditures, particularly on arms, the expansion of the post war decades can begin again, and that the problem of unemployment could thereby be solved.

★The economic theory behind this was first expounded by J.M. Keynes in the 1930s. Since then Keynesian economics has been in and out of favour as it tends not to be acceptable to right-wing governments. SC.

If the supposition is correct that mass unemployment is a permanent and not a temporary condition in many western countries – it is a legitimate question to ask if our thinking is ready to deal with the many consequences of such a condition. Are we prepared to take the steps that may be necessary? But the only idea as yet to have gained some currency is that everyone's hours should be reduced and the available work should be spread among the whole active population so that all who are able to work can have a paid job. This far from revolutionary thought meets with considerable opposition because of the enormous practical difficulties involved, and the unwillingness of many of those now working to give up any part of their salary, even if they do less work for it. But so long as pay and work remain so surely linked this probably remains the only possible solution.

So perhaps rather serious thought should be given to the alternative already mentioned: that none should be paid wages in exchange for work, but that *everyone* should receive a fair share of the available goods and resources. The idea of negative income tax has been widely discussed. Under such a scheme a particular sum would be designated as a poverty line, and anyone whose income fell below that would receive the difference from the state – which would have obtained the necessary funds through taxation. The principal objection to this idea was that negative income tax would encourage people who were capable of working for wages to work less, if at all. But since it has never been tried we cannot know what the effects would be. However, one can see that it would have the substantial advantage of being far less demeaning than registering for unemployment pay (puritans might think this a disadvantage, in that more people would be willing to register for money that it was their *right* to receive, and fewer would trouble to seek employment★).

★Such an effect would depend on the fine tuning of the scheme. In a tax-credit system, of which negative income tax is a part, incentives to engage in paid work arise, as now, out of people's desire to maximise their income. The tax credit system would be a substantial saver of administrative costs, and therefore of jobs also. SC.

It seems to me that without straight away going so far as to dissociate all work from wages, a combination of features from several plans might lead in the direction we have indicated earlier, at the same time as helping to solve many of the problems now facing the industrial world. A negative income tax would ensure that everyone, employed or not, had access to the basic necessities of life; the rest of the present system could remain intact. Work needed to provide goods and services for the whole population would be done by those who wanted more than the minimum, and they would be paid more or less as at present. By such means, absolute poverty – still to be found in many industrial countries – would have been abolished.

However, the major problem – ever fewer jobs available – would not be touched by this measure. Here I believe a leaf should be taken from Roosevelt's book. A first task would be the making of a comprehensive inventory of all the tasks that need to be done for the benefit of society that are not being done. For this kind of work, which might well be harder and more exacting than ordinary jobs performed by paid labour, only *volunteers* would be accepted. Although these volunteers would naturally come mainly from the ranks of the unemployed, others who wished to do it and were willing to accept only the payment provided through negative income tax would also be welcomed. Perhaps some prestige would come to be associated with such work, with one possible result being that gradually the citizenry might come to accept the notion that work should be done voluntarily and for the general benefit of mankind rather than for the personal benefit of the worker. And those who organize their work efficiently and competently would surely in time come to feel that they were helping mankind forward and this would and should be their major reward. However, if they begin to think that they have more difficult work and begin to compare what they do with what other workers do, they then might demand higher pay and that would be a sign that the system was not working as it should. But if workers come to wish above all to be more truly _satisfied_ by their work, it might be acceptable to forego surplus income for the sake of society and mankind. In such a case labour would cease to be a commodity to be bought and sold like things.

Earlier we raised the question of privilege – have we in any sense earned our privileged position? We did not attempt in this chapter to answer that question; but, it might equally well be asked: have we deserved to be given a fine, prestige-bearing, well paid job? Or, conversely, have we deserved to be unable to find any paid job at all? Those born to privilege, having done nothing in this life to have merited it, are obviously in an utterly different position. And unemployment is not necessarily a man's fault. The unemployed may fail to take advantage of opportunities offered, and many may be quite content with an education which could be much better. But some people also simply seem to suffer from bad luck when looking for jobs. Their own good qualifications may have been outshone by those of someone else who presented himself the same day. Their employer may have been forced to liquidate his business and let his employees go just at the time when there was a national depression.

All this comes within the framework of reincarnation and karma: our privileges or supposed ill-luck have to do with what is popularly called destiny. One cannot, of course, say why we are where we are, nor what it is that is required of us in this life – except in the most general terms. Even so I think it is of great value to try to explain in more detail what Steiner has taught on reincarnation and karma: how we progress through repeated earth lives and how we learn, both during our earthly lives and in a different way in our lives between death and rebirth. How at all times we are in the presence of invisible higher beings who are at hand to help us, and who aid in creating a destiny which we live out during our earthly incarnations. And, finally, how we can be free beings even though we are at the same time hedged about by circumstances we have chosen for ourselves. Such questions as these lead us into the very heart of anthroposophy. What we have thus far discussed and explored will provide a foundation for all that will be discussed in the next chapter on reincarnation and karma, when much that we have said ought to become clearer and fall into its proper place.

Chapter Six

Reincarnation and karma

IF THE INDIVIDUALITY that I call 'I' had come into being for the first time when I was in my mother's womb as an embryo, it is obviously logically impossible for me to have 'deserved' my parents. Nor could I have deserved the particular social milieu in which my parents moved, though it is possible to suppose, more logically, that my parents deserved to have a child like me. The common view is that as far as I myself am concerned, 'I' did not exist until the particular combination of genes and chromosomes united to form the embryo that later became 'me'. If these genes and chromosomes had been different, that is, if I had had a different parentage or had been born to the same parents at a different time, then I should have been born with entirely different qualities. The only reason I turned out to be as I was resulted from the original deed of my parents in coming together to procreate me.

According to this commonly accepted somewhat materialistic notion 'I' myself had nothing to do with my birth, and the fault or merit for having brought me into the world belongs to my parents. That I proved to be a burden and sore trial, or a joy and delight to them, might possibly have been due to good or bad qualities possessed by my father and mother, or, more probably, resulted from the way they brought me up. It is also possible to attribute my qualities to divine beings who provided me with my 'soul', if not with my body. But if my soul does indeed result from the work of divine beings and was created just at the time when my parents were coming together to create my body, as used to be the belief of Christians, then it becomes necessary to attribute my faults as well as my virtues to these same divine beings. So the question is bound to arise why I should have been gifted with the particular soul that I did indeed receive. Theologians have struggled with these problems from St. Augustine onward, but within the Church there is no really good logically and morally satisfying answer – none has as yet been provided either within the materialistic, or the traditionally Christian framework.

The materialistic scenario, moreover, provides no explanation at all as to how a being can come into existence from a combination of genes and chromosomes and nothing else, and yet call himself 'I'. On this view my 'I' must be identical with my body because nothing else exists but body. When my body comes into being as an embryo in my mother's womb, my 'I' presumably came into existence with it, and will be extinguished at death – unless of course there is a life after death for the soul when it has separated from the body. In general the materialists offer no explanation for the existence of the 'I', but also they do not find any need for one; it is not a problem. Their concept of the 'mind', by which they understand the activities of the human brain, includes the awareness of self, and as a rule they do not find it at all extraordinary that a small child should suddenly start to call himself 'I' without having ever been instructed to do so. For the materialists the human mind belongs to the human brain, and as the brain develops during childhood, at a certain moment the child will quite naturally say 'I' and no further explanations are necessary. For those who accept the idea of a soul of divine origin, at a certain moment in childhood the soul has so taken charge of the body that self-awareness and calling himself 'I' will naturally follow.

Such explanations as these seem to me to beg all the important questions. Is it after all so 'natural' for a being to possess speech, and be able to utter the word 'I' when no other creature in the world except man can do so? Or that 'self'-awareness should suddenly well up in a child of two or three years so that he calls himself by a word that no one else can use of him? Would not all the questions we have raised be satisfactorily answered if it were assumed that the human being has lived on earth before and is no stranger to it when he is born? That the being who calls himself 'I' has been on earth many times before but only becomes aware of himself as a separate entity about the age of three? That the position into which he is born is a result of what he has done during previous lives on earth? That he therefore has, in a very real sense, the parents he 'deserves' or needs and they have the children they also 'deserve'?

In our century very large numbers of western people have come to believe that we do not live only once, that we do indeed re-incarnate time and again in different epochs and to different parents. The concept of reincarnation seems to shed a new light on many problems. Many people believe they possess a very definite knowledge of former lives, and that they 'recognize' places they have never visited before in this life. Moreover the great majority of the world's peoples have always believed in reincarnation, including almost all peoples of the orient, and most people of Africa. Only the great monotheistic religions deny it, in large part because they enshrine beliefs regarding salvation in an afterlife that seem to be incompatible with the idea of repeated earth lives. However reincarnation alone does not answer by any means all of the questions we have raised; the popular ideas about reincarnation that in our time fill so many books leave most of the serious problems unanswered. The point is that the idea of karma* belongs with the idea of reincarnation; karma must

---

*Karma is a Sanskrit term for a principle of causality by which good and evil are believed to be merited by earlier deeds; good or bad karma can be built up through life. Karma is to be contrasted with the more familiar word destiny. The latter has a flavour of determinism whereas a person's karma arises out of his freely-chosen choices and actions. In anthroposophy the individual is seen as the architect of a series of life-courses which present opportunities that he may or may not grasp in the way 'required' by karma, if at all. sc.

be understood in as many of its nuances as possible. If at least the main features of karma, and in what respects it differs from mere destiny, are understood it will be seen how many questions are answered that quite legitimately are asked in our age of the consciousness soul. According to Steiner who devoted many hundreds of lectures to the subject of reincarnation and karma, the time has now come for western civilizations not only to accept and come to understand both, but also to understand how his teachings on the subject can be made an integral part of Christianity – even if such a Christianity is not what has been traditionally taught★. Here we shall try only to show how it is possible to reconcile karma with human freedom – and indeed how true human freedom cannot even be conceived of without an understanding of karma.

From the earliest time that man first incarnated in a human body he began to build karma for himself. His very first incarnation on earth provided him with karma for his next incarnation, and we have all been accumulating karma ever since. This karma is, with the aid of higher beings, elaborated between death and rebirth, but the deeds that create this karma have been performed only on earth. Between death and rebirth (when we are in the spiritual worlds and no longer have a body) we do not accumulate karma. When we are in our mother's womb we have brought our karma with us because karma is attached to our individuality, and we are already individualities as soon as we are conceived. During the ten lunar months before our birth we

★This subject is far too extensive to be treated in this modest book, and would involve, at the very least, a discussion of the nature of the second coming, the distinction between the day of death and what the Bible calls the Last Day. In what sense Christ redeemed all men from their sins, and how this is to be reconciled with our contention, in this chapter, that men compensate for their 'sins' in later lives – these are also subjects that would clearly have to be discussed at length. For these and other questions there is an excellent book by Rudolf Frieling entitled *Christianity and Reincarnation* (Edinburgh, Floris Books, 1977), which should be consulted by all those who wish to understand more fully how it can be that the teaching of reincarnation is entirely compatible with Christianity.

are building the physical, etheric, and astral bodies that we shall be using in the lifetime in front of us. At death, as was noted in an earlier chapter, we lay aside first the physical body, then, after about three days, our etheric body* which dissolves into the etheric world of formative forces. The astral body and ego then remain together for about a third of the period of the life just past – or, to put it another way, our ego remains with our astral body for about the same period as we spent in sleeping during this past life. Then the astral body also is dissolved, and the ego, always enriched by an extract of the experience of the past life and all previous ones, passes through the various spheres of the spiritual world until the time comes for it to incarnate once more.

The ego therefore is immortal. We always retain our individuality whether we are living on earth in a physical body or are in a spiritual, body-free existence between death and rebirth. Birth and death represent two great changes, from the spiritual to the physical (at birth), and from the physical to the spiritual (at death). There is nothing to be feared about either. It is one of Ahriman's legitimate tasks to see that we leave life when the time has come. But since one of his greatest weapons against man is to instil fear into him, Ahriman has also brought it about that we now, quite unnecessarily fear death. Pain, unlike death, may reasonably be feared. Before Ahriman was so active, and when human beings were clairvoyant, death was only a change in consciousness. Even today the Hindu people, whose religious tradition is still very much alive in them, celebrate death as the return of the soul and spirit to their real home after a period of travail and suffering within an earthly body. Modern men who, like William Blake, have been gifted with clairvoyance, have regarded death in a similar manner. Blake himself spoke of it as like going from one room into another.

It is the purpose of our lives on earth to make progress

*see earlier footnote on the various bodies, at the beginning of chapter two.

in spiritual development. Only relatively little can be achieved in this direction during a single lifetime, however packed with incident it may be. Therefore, it is essential for us all to be incarnated numerous times, and to have as wide an experience as possible from which to learn. With a few very rare exceptions human beings will continue to incarnate until that day in the far distant future when our planet, with our aid, will have attained its goal of becoming a cosmos of love. Love will then have been built into it, just as wisdom has been built into our present planet before it became our earth. Our lives therefore are not purposeless. Higher beings are deeply interested in all that we do. Each of the various hierarchies of spiritual beings above man have played, and continue to play, a part in man's development, but we are ordinarily unaware of them because it is necessary for us to experience freedom. So when we elaborate our karma between death and rebirth, with the aid of higher beings, we are creating a framework for our next life on earth, within which we shall feel we are free. And indeed we *are* free to do as we will, within this framework. The period we spend between death and rebirth is ordinarily several times longer than the period spent on earth in a physical body. During the entire period spiritual beings are working with us in constructing our karma – and indeed not only spiritual beings, but human beings with whom we are connected by our karma, share in the work. It is this karma that we bring with us when we are born, and in all its aspects it moulds the life we live, but we are free to act within this framework entirely in accordance with our will. How we use this freedom will of course determine in large measure the kind of incarnation we shall have in our next life on earth.

It should therefore be clear that reincarnation is simply a process that takes place for all of us. In contrast to karma it does not need to be explained, nor is it difficult to grasp. But the link between one life and subsequent ones; how our life dovetails with the lives of so many people with whom we spend our incarnation; how our deeds affect others and their deeds affect us; how it is possible to make progress by learning and experiencing from one incarnation to another – these things cannot be grasped, still less be easily understood. We may *believe* in reincarnation, but that belief by itself tells us only that we shall have another opportunity to make further progress and of course it should also take away any fear of death or of a last and final judgment. But it takes a long time and much effort before we begin to understand the many delicate ramifications of karma. These alone give meaning to the process of reincarnation. No more than a beginning can be made in this little book.

The workings of karma, as Steiner describes them, are truly wonderful and awe-inspiring. However many years we may spend in contemplating and trying to understand them, they always seem more wonderful than before. Indeed it is more than possible that such contemplations can succeed in convincing us that higher beings do exist, and are active in our lives. No *human* mind could have devised all those interconnections that we sometimes lazily call the workings of *chance*. Chance, indeed!

Let us take as an illustration all that had to happen in the earthly and heavenly worlds in order for me to be born to my parents, (or, for that matter, for others whom we know to be born to theirs). I was born in a cool northern climate in Europe to a couple that had been born in the same country but several hundred miles apart; born in that nation and race I had a white skin. But if, as I have said, our individualities are immortal, could I not equally well have been born in a different part of the world, with a black or brown skin? What was it that determined that I should be born as I was and in the particular social milieu in that cool northern country? Of course it was my karma. That is easy enough to say. I needed that particular race, nation and milieu if I were to fulfil the task I had set for myself as a result of my experiences in former earthly incarnations. Presumably I also needed the particular genes and chromosomes I found in my parents, or my physical and mental makeup would not have been precisely what I needed. How could I conceivably make such a choice all by myself, with the kind of mental capacities with which I entered the spiritual world after my last life on earth? And if, as Steiner says I did, I *chose* my own parents, what about them? Did they choose me? How could our respective choices be reconciled? Consciously, perhaps, one or both of them hoped to have a darling pretty little girl, and they got - me!

Now if we leave aside the notion of 'chance' – that is that there is no purpose behind these choices – and if we reject the notion that some omnipotent and all-wise God arranged it all, then I think it is reasonable that beings higher than man, perhaps great numbers of them, were responsible for bringing my parents together and seeing to it that I was born. These beings possessed faculties far more advanced than any that we can conceive of in connection with man, and were able to do all that was necessary. But granting all this, *why* should they do this for all human beings, everywhere? What kind of guidance did *they* need, and receive? The answer, as Steiner gives it, seems to me to be perfectly logical – and truly the only explanation that I find at all convincing: it was *we ourselves* who *chose* our destiny. But we did not, and could not, have chosen it alone. We needed the help of higher beings to enable our choice to be put into effect. We needed a superhuman knowledge, which we did not possess. If my parents were brought together, perhaps from widely separated parts of the world, they must of course have been linked by *their* karma. Could it have been I myself from the spiritual worlds who have brought them together so that I could be born? What kind of a superhuman knowledge could I have had to persuade my father and mother to meet, and perhaps *their* fathers and mothers before them, for several generations? What about my brothers and sisters, all waiting to be born to them, and likewise helping to bring them together?

Rudolf Steiner assures us that long before we incarnated we did indeed look down from the spiritual worlds, and with the aid of higher beings helped to weave all the webs of karma so that at last I and my brothers and sisters could be born within that family. Even if this involved bringing parents together from different continents the necessary karmic links would have to be forged or the final result – my own birth to those parents, and the birth of my brothers and sisters – would not have been possible. It may be conceded at once that only beings posssessed of an entirely different order of wisdom from ours could perform such a feat, and with our finite minds, even if we imagine the most advanced computer that could be made by man, we cannot imagine how it could be done. But when we have studied the way karma is created, and how it can be that we do choose our own karma, then we may find the process less incomprehensible.

The karma with which we were born, in addition to leading us to our chosen parents, brings about certain situations and events in our lives. It also causes us to meet those persons with whom we have a joint karma in this, and usually in future, lives on earth. However, we are also led by karma to meet other persons who were not karmically linked to us in the past, but with whom we shall be linked in the future. What we do together after our meeting, and how we act after a particular event brought about by karma lies within the realms of our freedom. The link from a previous life may involve a karmic obligation that is owed to us, or a debt that we ourselves owe. Whether and how this debt is repaid will have an influence in this life – if the debt, for example, is unpaid – *and* in the next. But we are not compelled by 'God' to make compensation, nor will a god punish us in this world, or the next, because of our deeds and of the debts we have incurred. It is *we* who decide in our life after death that we *wish* to make compensation for our deeds. And we reach this decision as the result of a crucial experience which we undergo soon after death.

It has been described in an earlier chapter how at death the etheric, astral body, and ego separate themselves from the physical body, and it is this indeed that we call death. The first experience we have immediately after death is a panorama of our whole life which unrolls backward from the moment of death to the moment of birth. Ordinarily this experience occupies about three days, at the end of which by far the greater part of our etheric body returns to the etheric world from which it originally came, leaving only the smallest 'extract' of it, in effect that part of it that has been transformed and perfected by our 'I' in the course of our life, to progress onward with our astral body and 'I'.

Our astral body and 'I' now enter a region which has become known in anthroposophy as kamaloka*, an echo of which is to be found in the Catholic concept of 'purgatory'. Our period in kamaloka lasts for about a third of the time we spent on earth. This is not arbitrary – we spend about a third of our life in sleeping, and what is experienced during this period is a recapitulation of our experiences during sleep, which are indeed a foretaste of kamaloka. In our sleep and in kamaloka we experience what we have done to our fellow-men as if it had been done to *us*. If we struck someone during the day or harboured thoughts of hatred towards them, then in the following night we experience, in the unconsciousness of sleep, that blow and those thoughts of hatred, as if we were their victims. Also during our sleep higher beings who are concerned with us look down and, to use Steiner's words, 'rain down' their approval or disapproval on us. What we experience in this way during the night lives half conscious in us the following day in the form of *conscience*.

Kama-loka is a Sanskrit term, the *lokas* of the Hindu system are a range of regions (some material, the *rupa-lokas;* the others spiritual, the *arupa-lokas*) set aside for specific purposes. SC.

Our conscience is very far from being what Freud supposed. It is not just a 'superego' made up of dictates arising out of our treatment in childhood by our parents, teachers and others who have had authority over us. It is not only our own, half-conscious, knowledge of the evil we have done and the good we have failed to do, but it is also knowledge that has been built into us by the approval or disapproval of higher beings. The experience remains in our waking life just below the threshold of consciousness. When after death we experience the panorama of our lives we are not hindered by our body as we are in life. So we experience all the events of our life in the utmost clarity, and the memory of them remains vivid during the whole period of kamaloka. The experience of our nights on earth, arising from this memory tableau, is now re-lived with a similar clarity. All the harm we have done to our fellow beings, every unhappiness we have caused them, is lived through again within our own self – as is also the good we have done, and the happiness for which we have been responsible. But the evil we have done causes us, in the depths of our being, to wish to compensate for it. Our resolve to make this compensation is heard by the higher beings who are concerned with us, and it is they who help to fulfil it.

Although karmically we are linked in one lifetime with relatively few human beings (and we shall meet these individualities again in our next life), it is only very rarely that we shall have the same relationship with them. It is evident why this should be so: it is necessary for us over the course of our incarnations to have entirely different experiences if we are to learn something different from each. For example, it is usual for a male to be a female in the next incarnation, and vice versa. In this way it becomes possible to balance the experience of masculinity and femininity; the two experiences are obviously complementary. We all need both if we are to make progress. It is especially salutary to consider that if we have been aggressively masculine or feminine in one incarnation we shall subsequently be born with the opposite sex, and may well suffer by being unable to perform our proper task because of the dislike we formerly had for the sex we shall then have. If we are aggressively masculine in this incarnation this may be because previously we were unable adequately to carry out the role of a woman. Every life is in sense a metamorphosis of our last one as well as being a preparation for the next. But this does not mean that the roles of husband and wife, or son and mother or other similar relationships are reversed next time. We are unlikely to have the same life partner, though he or she may now be a close relative, a brother or sister, a parent; or even a close friend or business associate. Steiner who through his supra-sensible faculties was able to investigate and record successive incarnations of various historical personages, mentions a few cases of masters and slaves whose roles were later reversed, and teachers who later became pupils of men who had been their own pupils in a former life.

However, these rather obvious instances of metamorphosis and compensation do not seem to be the rule. Most of the cases investigated by Steiner could never have been predicted, nor what form the necessary metamorphoses would take. For this reason, if for no other, it is wise to be extremely wary of the many supposed instances of reincarnation described by respectable psychologists and psychiatrists who have reported discovering through hypnosis and other methods the previous incarnations of their patients*. It is remarkable in these cases how often these patients have the same or similar relationships with the same person (so that there is no real metamorphosis), and the stories uncovered are often so easily predictable that they carry no conviction to an anthroposophist who reads of them. The

*Even otherwise respectable anthroposophists have not always refrained from speculating on these matters, but their speculations are not necessarily worth any more than those of the non-anthroposophist. As far as I am aware no anthroposophist, other than Rudolf Steiner, has ever achieved the degree of development necessary for this kind of investigation.

previous lives 'revealed' by the hypnotist or psychiatrist could have been unconsciously 'suggested' to the patient because the therapist was looking for an explanation from a previous life to account for the symptoms observable in this one. Or the patient could himself have woven the story in much the same way that plausible dreams are so often woven from quite ordinary earthly happenings although nothing really happened in life in the way the dream reveals it. The point is that nothing is really *revealed* by what the therapists often call 'far memory'. The usually banal stories teach absolutely nothing about the real relationship between a past life and the present one, or at least nothing that could not have been easily invented by either the therapist or the patient. Moreover, for what that may be worth, the supposed reincarnations are ordinary far too close in time to be in accord with Steiner's descriptions of the norm in the cases he investigated*.

Lastly – and this assertion cannot of course be directly verified without suprasensible perception – it is also possible for mischievous elemental beings (whose existence has until very recent times always been known) who are not at present incarnated in human bodies, to insert themselves into the astral bodies of persons in a state of trance, or other abnormal conditions of consciousness. Such elemental beings are able to suggest replies to the therapist that supposedly come from their patients, with the sole purpose of deceiving him. I wish to emphasize as strongly as I can that Steiner always insisted that it is extremely difficult to investigate former incarnations of anyone. And the most difficult of all to investigate would be one's own. For reasons that it is not necessary to go into now it is likely that human beings in the coming centuries will be able to percieve and

*There is no real norm; the period between incarnations has varied greatly over the course of history. Steiner has given a few examples of incarnations very close in time, but these were very special cases, usually requied by world Karma. Ordinarily, even in modern times, at least a few centuries elapsed between incarnations and this interval should be generally regarded as the most probable.

remember their own former incarnations; but it will never be a simple matter to reach any certainty as to whether it is one's own incarnation that one is actually experiencing. It could quite as easily be the incarnation of someone else closely linked with us by his karma.

Karma and freedom

This chapter will be concluded by trying to answer the question with which we started it, namely how far we have 'merited' our good fortune in being born in one of the privileged nations of the west. But before dealing with that we must look at the obvious and perfectly reasonable question: how can we be said to be free, and free to pursue the human goal of freedom of which we have spoken, if we are *condemned* to compensate for our former actions on earth? How can we be free if all our relationships are determined in advance – if we are not free, for example, to meet new people whom we might well have preferred to our actual karmic companions? Even if we have ourselves chosen, when in the spiritual worlds, to compensate for our former deeds on earth because we came to understand their consequences, does not karma greatly limit all our possibilities in this life? Therefore is not our supposed freedom more or less of an illusion?

In answer to these questions it must be emphasized first of all that our karma only leads us to the necessary meeting with a person with whom we have a karma to fulfil. This meeting is never arranged by ourselves. It is arranged by higher beings who are concerned with us and our life, especially by that being who has always been known as our guardian angel. He it is above all who brings us together with the person whom we must meet; and of course he acts in cooperation with the angel of the other person. Once we have met, we are *now* free to behave towards that other person *exactly as if* no previous karma existed between us. The kind of relationships we have with him will be our own doing, and we shall experience them as such, and feel no constraint imposed on us by our karma.

Let us take as an example a husband and wife relationship. If in this life we have chosen to marry and live out our lives together, this common life will take a particular form because of our need to fulfil the karma we have brought over from previous lives. But *in this life* we are both of us at all times free to act towards one another as our freedom dictates, not under any compulsion from karma. We may be unhappy in this relationship; that unhappiness may result from the fact that we are not resolving those problems we have brought over from a past life. Or, by contrast, because of what we do this time we may indeed complete fruitfully what we brought over from before. In both instances we experience ourselves in this life as subjectively free to do as we wish. Our knowledge of the fact of karma in no way impairs this freedom, but it does help us to understand why things so often turn out in a way we had not expected. In particular we may be able to understand why something into which we have put all our efforts may for no obvious apparent reason fail, and not at all because we did not try hard enough. Though we cannot of course understand the karmic details behind our failure, it is often wonderfully consoling if we can bring ourselves to accept such a failure with equanimity instead of trying to force events to conform to our wishes. When our efforts to accomplish something become counter-productive, as they so often do, that is clear evidence that we were not *intended* to do it, and the effort surely should be abandoned.

In practical life it requires much thought, effort and experience over many years before we can determine with any degree of certainty whether or not an event is of a karmic nature, and whether a particular human relationship is a purely casual one, or arises from the depths of our karma. The opportunities for deceiving ourselves are so many that we may sometimes conclude that it would have been better for us never to have heard of karma rather than to try to explain too many things by it. But it is at all times an excellent exercise to try to view our own actions as if they had been performed by someone else, and this may be a useful corrective when we are inclined to make excuses for our own actions. If, for example, we grow tired of our wife or of our husband and find a more than acceptable alternative, we may 'decide' that our karma with our present spouse is over and that we have both learned all the lessons from it that we can. It may seem that a new karma is about to begin, and if we fail to co-operate in making a change-over that is willed by our karma we shall be making a serious mistake, and not grasping an opportunity provided for us by our angel! Such arguments may appear particularly convincing if we seem to have been led to our proposed new partner by very tortuous paths of destiny that we could never have arranged for ourselves. Perhaps the new meeting does have a karmic background; perhaps we do have some karma to fulfil with the person we have just met. But it is not necessarily the case that the particular kind of relationship we are now envisaging is the one that will be best for us both, and for our existing partner, whom we are proposing to abandon. It is very dangerous to jump to conclusions in such matters. From the moment of meeting the person to whom we feel an 'instinctive' and possibly karmic sympathy (or antipathy) we are totally free to make our decisions on the basis of all those factors that we should take into consideration if we had no knowledge of karma. In other words, an almost infinite number of possibilities exist for making a new relationship fruitful, and these we must explore just as if we were ignorant of karma. The only difference, and it should be a crucial one, is that we have the knowledge that the relationship is one that requires our earnest attention and the best thought we can give to it. It has been sent to us for a purpose, and did not come about by 'chance', so we explore it and do not pass it by.

It is always worth remembering Steiner's statement in the last chapter of his book *Theosophy* that sympathy and antipathy should become for us the 'eyes of the soul'. If we experience immediate sympathy or antipathy for someone, we should be able to *perceive* that person better, and even more clearly because of the instant of attention we gave to him without our willing it. Through our sympathy or antipathy we ought to be able also to learn something about ourselves, and what it was in us, as well as in them, that attracted or repelled us. All life ought to be a means for the enrichment of our experience – nothing is ever learned from indifference. And while all human relationships cannot be equally fruitful for us, all can in some degree enrich both ourselves and those with whom we come in contact. If we know, or even suspect, that karma lies behind any particular meeting; that this karma demands to be fulfilled and that it needs our conscious participation, then it will surely make our life more meaningful. We are on earth as social beings, and it is in company with others that we tread our life-path. But since nothing is gained by indifference and inattention, so also nothing is gained by self-deception. That indeed may well lead to a bitter experience of frustration, especially if it is ultimately realized that something more fruitful could have been attained, and we lost it through our own fault and neglect.

Let us look at some other events that may come out of karma. Serious accidents are almost invariably karmic in origin. Especially in the later part of our lives they can prove to be hard trials, the successful overcoming of which may bear fruit in later lives. All we can do about them is accept them with fortitude and equanimity. Our knowledge of karma may help us not to complain of our ill fortune, and especially not to blame other people (even though they may be actually responsible for them directly in this life) nor blame divine beings, who may indeed have brought them about for our ultimate good. In his book *Manifestations of Karma* Steiner has given us much information about the karmic reasons for certain accidents, and these we do not need to repeat here. We may have been led to an accident because the accident and its numerous consequences constituted the only, or at least the best, way for us to receive a lesson that we needed because of events in a former life. Only through the suffering arising from the accident could we have learned this particular lesson. If others were involved in the accident, it may have been necessary for us to tie ourselves very closely in karma with the others, and perhaps especially with the person responsible for it, who will have incurred a karmic debt that will some day have to be repaid. This link may have come from a former life, or it may forge a connection for the future. It is impossible for us to tell which; sometimes it can even be an event that forms a bridge between a past life and a future one. Again it is our task to take what fruits we can from the experience; and we should, at least when we have recovered from its effects, make a serious attempt to understand it, and see how we have after all been able to grow as a result of the experience.

Similar considerations apply to illnesses – except that by no means all illnesses are karmic in origin. In other words, they may not have resulted from deeds or attitudes in a former life. On this also Steiner had much to say, but all we need do here is indicate a few of the possibilities. A disease may come from actions and attitudes in this present life which work themselves out at a later period of our lives, and, so to speak, cleanse us of what we might have had to suffer in a subsequent life. The way in which we endure our illnesses may bear fruit not only in this life but in also the next. Illnesses accompanied by high fevers may greatly strengthen us, if we can survive the illness and do not succumb to it. Modern fever therapy which makes use of antibiotics to prevent us not only from succumbing but even from having the disease in a serious way at all, is not necessarily good for us in the long run. For it is true that if we avoid suffering that comes to us out of karma, it is only too probable that we will have to suffer in a different way later. The same problem very often presents itself in a different manner, and sooner or later we are required to deal with it, either in this or subsequent lives. This observation is not intended to counsel against using antibiotics and other modern means available to us for avoiding suffering. But it remains true that we should not have recourse to such aids *as a matter of course* simply because they are available. We may also *think* whether or not we wish to make use of them in a particular case. Tentative and uncertain as our conclusions must necessarily be, we ought not simply to forget all we know about karma and leave it out of consideration. Least of all should we at the onset of an illness at once forget everything we know and have learned simply because our own beloved body is involved!

Karma and privilege

We will now return to the subject with which we began this chapter: why should we have been privileged to be born in the relatively comfortable society in which we find ourselves? What, if anything, have we done to deserve it? If we have indeed merited our privileges, when and how did we come to earn them?

It is of course impossible to give answers to these questions that would be applicable in all cases. But what we have said about karma should indicate in what direction an answer is to be found. All of us have reached a certain point in our journey, with many incarnations behind us and many still to come. Like all other human beings we have a double task on earth, to develop ourselves and to place all we have learned and achieved at the disposal of our fellow-men and the world in which we all live. We cannot *learn* in the spiritual worlds. In order to learn we need to be incarnated in a physical body, and undergo the experiences possible only when we are on earth. Over all our lifetimes we need a very great variety of experiences, and for this reason will surely incarnate in many different societies. If we have been born this time in an American or European body, this will be because only in such a body can we learn what it is in our karma to learn this time. None of us can hope to make an uninterrupted progress in our development, and in any event our progress will take on a different colouring according to whether we have been born as a boy or girl. We ourselves might only rarely choose the particular milieu into which we were born, if we made a conscious choice while on earth. As we have tried to make clear we simply do not now know just what is good for us. Neither do we know in what position we can best serve mankind; divine beings may well wish us to spend an incarnation in a lowly position (as the world regards such things) in order to undergo certain experiences that may be useful for us and for others – either in that incarnation or later – after our experiences have been lived through again in the spiritual worlds.

The matter of crucial importance is what we do with the privileges, if such they are, with which we have been born. Nothing, according to the anthroposophical view, has been given to us simply to *enjoy*. It has often been observed how frequently, for example, a person who has inherited great wealth is not made at all happy by it. Such an inheritance is in fact a heavy responsibility and in itself may be the direct cause of much unhappiness and frustration. An heiress is never certain whether she is loved for herself or for her money, she is likely to be set upon by numerous fortune hunters and confidence men, never knowing whom she can trust. She will surely receive numerous begging letters from strangers and requests for financial help or financial backing from her friends, and even from distant acquaintances. If she wishes to use her money wisely and responsibly, then she is sure to have to make agonizing decisions which may cause her considerable distress. It may be only a very small compensation that she can apparently do as she likes, that she can buy anything that takes her fancy, and does not have to work for a living. It may indeed be that such a person was greedy and avaricious, or unloving and selfish in a previous life, and *she* had to learn in this one how little joy the inherited possessions *he* had sought last time would now mean to him when in his new incarnation he actually had them at his disposal. If we simply accept our life as it has been given to us and enjoy our privileges, if we even thank 'God' for them but do nothing truly useful for the world with them, then we are wasting the opportunity we have been granted. And it is certain that our subsequent lives will be affected by the negative karma we shall have built up during this one.

The greatest benefit we can obtain for ourselves from our knowledge of karma is being able to accept whatever happens to us without wishing that things were different. In one of his lectures Steiner gave us a picture that carries with it an important lesson. He imagined a man who "climbs on a roof, quickly loosens a tile, but only to the point where it still has a certain hold: then he runs quickly to the ground so that when the tile has become quite detached it falls on his shoulders", injuring him★. The tile did not fall by 'chance', but as a result of his own action. He has no one to blame for it but himself. So it is in life. The falling tile or any other untoward event is something he himself willed before birth. This event was chosen by higher beings as a fulfilment of what he had willed, and it was they who guided him to it. If we are passed over for promotion or someone else is given a job on which we had set our heart, we must learn to say to ourselves that it was his karma that was working when his employer singled him out for it, and that it is our karma that we did not get it. So immediately it becomes our task to see what more there is in our present job that we have not extracted from it, what opportunity may lie hidden in it that we have not yet seen. Even if we lose a job and become

★Steiner, R: *Reincarnation and Karma, their Significance in Modern Culture,* Vancouver, Steiner Book Centre, 1977; lecture of 20 February 1912.

unemployed we must always ask ourselves what can be wrung, for our benefit and for the benefit of the world, out of our enforced leisure, or out of an apparently dull and un-rewarding job that we are forced to take. Such a statement is intended to be taken seriously. It is not offered as a mere consolation for disappointment. Disappointments of this kind are of great significance in our lives and we may often learn more from studying them than from rejoicing over any of our successes.

Similarly with other apparent setbacks, whether they come to us through our fault, or apparently by someone else's fault. A person we loved and were sure we wanted to marry and would have been happy with, preferred to marry someone else. This choice he or she was free to make. And if in our hearts we accept it as such, almost surely the time will come when we see that there were many and important compensations in it for us, and after all we may come to think we should not have been happy together. But it is also possible that either we or the other person made a mistake, and it was intended that we should have married and lived our lives together. In another life on earth a similar decision with the same individuality may be planned for us, and then perhaps we can make the right choice for us both. Karma, we wish to emphasize again, is neither destiny nor fate. In our age it is necessary that we should be free also to make mistakes, and sometimes to make the wrong decision even after our joint karma has brought us together.

So we return to the point at which we started in this chapter. Every privilege with which we have been gifted is both a challenge and an opportunity. This time our privi-lege may be very great, and not necessarily because we have earned it nor because we have worked ourselves up to this high and privileged position. We may have gained it because higher beings, who know us infinitely better than we know ourselves (and know also all our previous lives on earth), have decided that this is the position in which we can best fulfil our Karma. As we have seen, this Karma we have created for ourselves in our former lives, and the position into which we have been born may also be one in which we can help humanity onward if we wish to and have the necessary will and determination. If we do all that we can in this position, then it may be that even more and greater opportunities will come our way next time.

But whether that will mean another life in an apparently privileged position it is not for us to decide. All we can know for certain from our knowledge of reincarnation and karma is that nothing we do is meaningless or without consequence. And, as we pass from incarnation to incarnation and on into the future, nothing is lost. In spite of the hardships that may be ours at a particular moment, we can take courage from the knowledge that, as Lessing put it, 'all eternity is mine' and we can feel confidence in life and work positively towards the goals we set ourselves before we were born but which we can come to know only in the course of our life.

Epilogue

What of the future?
The significance of Steiner's work

IN THIS BOOK no attempt has been made to minimize the dangers facing mankind, dangers which certainly become no less menacing in the light of the study of anthroposophy. But as students of this science perhaps we also find more grounds for encouragement than if we look at the world from the point of view of materialism – even traditional Christianity gives mankind no great encouragement to believe in a much better future on earth. But Steiner's vision of the task of mankind includes the possibility of bringing this task to fulfilment.

It has not been the purpose of this book to go in any great detail into the work of Rudolf Steiner, nor is this epilogue a suitable place for it. What I wish to do here is rather to stress once again the purpose and mission of man as it was envisaged by Steiner, thus placing in perspective the time of troubles in which we are at present engulfed. Steiner's vision was not an apocalyptic one. He did not predict disaster or destruction for mankind. But he warned that if men continued to abuse their freedom and continued to follow only the dictates of materialism and self interest; if they remained blind and deaf to what the science of spirit had to tell them about the non-material world and its beings, then disaster *was* possible, and it would not be averted by the intervention of divine spiritual beings. Men are now free, must take the consequences, and not expect to be saved from their folly.

According to Steiner, man is essentially a spiritual being who belongs to the physical world only in his body, the only part of him that is made up of earthly substances. From the moment of conception he begins to combine earthly substances and adds and exchanges these substances all his life. At death he casts them all off, and at once they begin to decay and return to the earth from which they came. Man's task on the earth is to learn everything that can be learned from living in a body; it is, indeed, only on the earth that he can learn. In the spiritual worlds between incarnations he experiences the life he has just lived from a spiritual point of view, and understands it. He prepares there the kind of life (including the kind of physical body) that will be most helpful for his spiritual growth.

However, man is not isolated on earth or in the universe. The universe is peopled by innumerable spiritual beings, including nine great hierarchies above man, each of which has its own task to perform. There are also elemental beings of all kinds, including some that are in the service of evil powers who are intent on preventing man, the tenth hierarchy, from attaining his goal and thus fulfilling the task he was set in the beginning. At the present time all these beings are invisible to man, they cannot be apprehended by any of our ordinary physical senses. The only kingdoms that are visible to us are those of minerals, plants, animals and our fellow human beings, since all these possess physical bodies.

To perceive the other beings of which we have spoken it is necessary to develop higher faculties than those with which we were born, that is suprasensible faculties. These faculties used to belong to man as a natural endowment, and will do so again in the not so far distant future. Meanwhile they can be developed only by human beings who have made preparation in many earlier lives, and who follow a path of higher development such as that described by

Rudolf Steiner in his book *Knowledge of the Higher Worlds*. These men are destined to become the leaders of humanity in our age, though very few of them work openly in the world. Rudolf Steiner felt it to be his task to make known to his fellow-men the truths about the spiritual world and spiritual beings that they need at the present moment. Especially in the last years of his life he made use of his spiritual knowledge in indicating new paths for humanity to follow in the arts and sciences. Enough work has been done by his followers and successors to show that this spiritual knowledge (at least in these fields) was well founded, that it was not mere theory or speculation, but could lead to practical results in earthly life.

The possession of spiritual knowledge, whether we acquire it for ourselves, or accept it from Rudolf Steiner or others, carries certain responsibilities with it. At the very least we ought always to be consciously aware of the spiritual around us, and of our own higher being, which is spiritual in nature. We cannot therefore live as if we were simply more developed animals coming into existence for the first time at conception and becoming totally extinguished at death. Having learned about reincarnation and karma from Rudolf Steiner it becomes impossible for us to spend our lives concerned only with material things and ephemeral earthly relationships; and having heard from him about the true significance for earth evolution of the life of Christ we cannot act as if there were no beings in the universe higher than ourselves, who are deeply concerned with man and wish for him to reach his goal of becoming free, and through freedom build love, the fruit of freedom, into the world. The knowledge that Steiner brought to mankind is intended to fire our *wills,* so that our deeds will be different because of this knowledge.

It is with this knowledge in our hearts that we should look upon the world and our fellow-men. Then we recognize the same spark of divinity that is in us, the same 'I' as the central core of their being, each with the same potentiality for being filled with the impulse of Christ. Filled with this awareness of the other person, we cannot treat any human being like a *thing,* or like an animal, to be enslaved or made to do our will. Nor can we look upon the earth as if it were nothing but so much raw material for us to use, as we see fit. The earth too is only the outward manifestation of the spiritual, as we are ourselves, and it is filled with beings towards whom we have a duty, as we have to our fellow-men.

So when we come to understand, for example, what lies behind the biodynamic farming (one of Steiner's greatest gifts to mankind), or why in the Steiner Schools he founded the effort is made to help every single child to develop his or her individuality; or why Steiner valued so highly even the most retarded or handicapped child (handicapped or retarded only in this single incarnation) and through his curative education began a whole new movement which has spread throughout the world; it can readily be seen that his practical work in the world, which has borne such fruit, and is bearing such fruit, rested on his spiritual knowledge and understanding of the task of man.

Once Steiner spoke of man as being 'the *religion* of divine beings', the '*religion* of the gods'. This tremendous saying, which it is possible to begin to understand only after decades of pondering on it, tells us something we could not have discovered for ourselves, nor would we have dared to proclaim it if the thought had occurred to us. It says nothing less than that our task as men is so highly valued by divine beings, they are so much concerned with us, that they bestow on us the kind of reverence that we ourselves offer to the divine world. They recognize, as we ourselves cannot do, that when man was created he was to be granted freedom, something enjoyed by no other species in the universe. Not only are plants and animals made to be exactly what they are, with no possibility of freeing themselves from the divine will, but higher beings also are not permitted by their very nature to do as they wish. They must obey the divine will too, even the hindering beings of whom we have spoken, whose allotted task is to tempt man, and who carry out this task only by divine permission.

But *our* freedom as men is real. It was a tremendous risk that higher powers took when they made it possible – with the greatest difficulty and through the cooperation of innumerable spiritual beings – for man to be endowed with freedom, which included the freedom to destroy the earth and all his fellow human beings. Even so this freedom, which was actually the gift of Lucifer, one of the two great hindering powers, would have led to nothing but egotism if the highest spiritual being who takes part in earthly evolution had not sacrificed himself by taking on a physical body and then experiencing in his own being what no other divine being had ever experienced. Through his sacrificial death and resurrection Christ also endowed man with this possibility of *self*less love. It is this potentiality for loving that came to man through the Christ that makes man worthy of the reverence that higher beings pay to him, for they themselves, having no freedom, cannot love in the same way as man.

This at least is what I personally understand by the astounding sentence quoted above. And I picture these divine beings and their leader, the Christ, looking down on men and wondering whether after all men may not have been given too much freedom and too much responsibility. And wondering also if the great experiment, the greatest that has ever been undertaken in the history of our solar system, may fail. Divine beings can stand ready to help, but they cannot take over any of the responsibility themselves, because if they did we should not be truly free. Man, without freedom, could not be man as the divine beings intended him to be, and this is the inescapable truth and the inescapable dilemma.

EPILOGUE

At the present moment the future scarcely looks auspicious. Men and women do not appear to be hungry and thirsty for spiritual knowledge – or far too few of them. They may possess excellent impulses, and wish to the very best of their capacities to help humanity. But without the vision that belongs to the science of spirit it is not possible to see the whole, nor to recognize what part our own work plays in it. We may cultivate our garden with the utmost enthusiasm and dedication, and this work may even be magnificent. But the whole is more all-encompassing than even the largest of our gardens, or even all gardens put together. It is this vision that I have wished to place in front of all of you who have made this journey with me – in the hope that with understanding will come the will to work, not only for yourselves, your own family, nation and race, but for the whole of endangered humanity – endangered perhaps now as it never has been before at any time in the past.

Suggestions for further reading

For additional reading on the subjects covered in this book the most practical recommendation I can make is to refer to my book *Man and World in the Light of Anthroposophy* (2nd edit., Anthroposophic Press, 1982), which contains an annotated reading list at the end of each chapter, something difficult to find in any other book published in English. Since each chapter is devoted to a particular topic, works by Steiner and others that cover this topic can easily be found. Moreover there is a detailed index from which the relevant chapter can be ascertained.

All Steiner's basic books are likely to prove helpful. The two most important and informative of these are called *Theosophy* (1904) and *Occult Science: an Outline* (1909) both available in many different editions. Equally fundamental but more in the nature of instructions for self-training are *The Philosophy of Freedom* (1894) and *Knowledge of the Higher Worlds and its Attainment* (1904). If someone works through the first-named slowly and thoroughly he is likely to find that he has not only begun to train his thinking but will have acquired an understanding of the nature of freedom unlike his former notion of it, and he will probably be stimulated to undertake further work in this realm on his own. *Knowledge of the Higher Worlds* is a perennially popular book which shows the reader the steps to be taken to develop his own character, and incidentally how if he perseveres long enough he can attain true higher development. Reading and working with the *Philosophy of Freedom* is itself an aid to such development along the path of thinking, whereas merely to read *Knowledge of the Higher Worlds* will achieve nothing. To profit from it the student must follow Steiner's instructions, not for a limited time only, but for the rest of his life.

Most of Steiner's lecture cycles and courses presuppose a certain familiarity with his fundamental teachings and are usually devoted to some special topic. A noteworthy exception is a cycle called *Rosicrucian Esotericism* (Anthroposophic Press, 1978) which was given at a Theosophical Congress held at Budapest in 1909. The audience, made up of members of the Theosophical Society, had for the most part little knowledge of what Steiner, then the general secretary of the German Section of the Theosophical Society, was teaching in Germany and on lecture tours abroad. So he evidently prepared this cycle as a kind of brief summary of the basic elements of his teachings which were later to be given the name of anthroposophy. As a summary it is still useful because of its exemplary clarity, though of course it is no substitute for a study of the basic books themselves. Three lectures given in Copenhagen in 1911 to the Scandinavian Theosophical Society Steiner thought so likely to be useful for beginners that he revised them for publication, something almost unique in his lecturing career. The title *The Spiritual Guidance of Man and Humanity* sufficiently describes their content and their relevance to the general theme of this book (Anthroposophic Press, 1983).

On the problem of evil discussed in Chapter 3 there is a valuable short study by Alfred Schütz, a Christian Community priest, which takes into account more of what Steiner had to say about Lucifer and Ahriman than was possible in this book. This work is entitled *The Enigma of Evil* (Edinburgh Floris Books, 1978). Two short cycles by Steiner, both published by Steiner Book Centre, Vancouver (*Influences of Lucifer and Ahriman,* 1919, and *The Balance in World and Man,* 1914) give much information on the subject, but some anthroposophical background is needed if they are to be understood. Unfortunately, on the evolution of consciousness, a key concept of Steiner, nothing by him can be recommended for the beginner. The book republished in 1966 under the title *The Evolution of Consciousness* has almost nothing on the subject. This cycle delivered in Penmaenmawr in 1923 was originally called *The Evolution of the World and of Humanity,* and this title was much more apposite. The evolution of consciousness was only touched upon right at the end. I can suggest only the long chapter two of my book *Man and World..* to be followed by Steiner's Stuttgart cycle of 1910 entitled *Occult History* (Rudolf Steiner Press, 1983), and other works mentioned in the reading list for this chapter. However there is also a most stimulating work by Owen Barfield called *Saving the Appearances* which deals with this subject from a totally different point of view, arriving by his own path at similar conclusions to Steiner's.

For Rudolf Steiner's ideas on the social order the fundamental book which became a best seller following World War 1 is at present available in English under two different titles: *Towards Social Renewal* (Rudolf Steiner Press, 1977) and *The Threefold Social Order* (Anthroposophic Press, 1972). The last named is slightly abridged. Although Steiner gave many more specialized lectures on several of the subjects discussed in that work, and some of these are available in English, the more general lectures given in Zurich in 1919 and published under the title *The Social Future* (Anthroposophic Press, 1972) will probably be the most useful for the average reader.

On the subject of reincarnation and karma there is a clear and simple single lecture given by Steiner in Vienna in 1912 called *Facing Karma* (Anthroposophic Press, 1975) and a relatively easy cycle full of information on karma as a general principle called *Manifestations of Karma* given in Hamburg in 1910 (Rudolf Steiner Press, 1976). Among the numerous lectures afterwards given by Steiner on the subject the lectures given in Berlin and Stuttgart in 1912, and published under the title *Reincarnation and Karma: Their Significance in Modern Culture* (Vancouver: Steiner Book Centre, 1977) are very helpful and easily comprehensible. More advanced students may wish to deepen their knowledge by studying some of the lectures given by Steiner in the last year of his life and published in eight volumes by Rudolf Steiner Press from ·1966 onwards. The collective title of the series is *Karmic Relationships*. The first six lectures of Vol. 1 and Lectures 18 to 28 of Vol. 2 deal with karma in general, without the specific examples given in most of the other lectures of this series. On life between death and rebirth the 1914 cycle given in Vienna entitled *The Inner Nature of Man and Life Between Death and Rebirth* is the most comprehensive cycle on the subject, and its two introductory lectures for the public are masterpieces of clarity (forthcoming from Rudolf Steiner Press). The short cycle called *Supersensible Man* given at the Hague in 1923 is a indispensable supplement to the Vienna cycle, but it goes without saying that Chapters 2 and 3 of the fundamental book *Theosophy* should have been mastered before undertaking either of these more esoteric cycles.

Lastly I should like to draw attention to the books written by Mary Caroline Richards and published by Wesleyan University Press, in which many anthroposophical themes are discussed in somewhat the same vein as in the present book, and of course in the light of a thoroughly assimilated anthroposophy. Among these books should be mentioned *Crossing Point, Centering,* and *Toward Wholeness*.